STILL LIFE
w/ extras

Maiche Lev

STILL LIFE
w/ extras

by Maiche Lev
All Rights Reserved
Copyright © 2018 HDW Publications

Cover and book design by David Bricker

ISBN:978-0-9975757-3-6

http://www.maichelev.com

Set List

STILL LIFE

with extras

Of some success
There is born an insatiable greed
Always this comes back
To bite you on the ass

PORCH SONG

You might think it a worthwhile pastime
To chat it up about your friends
You know, to your brother or your sister
Tyin' up loose ends
It may be something juicy
Like a ripe piece of melon
Sittin' fat there on the porch
Just drippin' for the tellin'

It may be your habit at get-togethers
To sit around and shoot the shit
You know, exaggerating the facts some
Sprucin' things up a bit
Come to think of it, nothin' really wrong with it
That is, of course, whether or not you take
    under consideration
What becomes of any truth
From this charmed, gloating wit

It's called 'evil speech' by scholars
Past and present
Present and past
A lot of hot air
He plays the fool

She holds her tongue
Hot air
Somebody's mistress
Somebody's heir

It's nice to have something to say
Over coffee or tea
Maybe even to write a letter
'Serendipity'
How heinous, the very notion
To share openly what has come between two…
What does gossiping make you?
But a maker of scenes
To a scene-making crew

You might think it a worthwhile pastime
To chat it up about your friends
You know, to your brother or your sister
Tyin' up loose ends
It may be something juicy
Like a ripe piece of melon
Sittin' fat there on the porch
Just drippin' for the tellin'

WHEN I THINK OF YOU

When I think of you
I don't think of where y' been
I think of your shoulders
Your look
Your gaze
Your person

When I think of you
I see the part in your hair
Your copper eyes, lit
I'm with you
We're somewhere
I'm sure of it

When I think of you
I know I failed to make a friend
I failed to make a friend
Of someone meant to be
More than a friend

How many times have I found the rope's end?
A dyin' voice within
The price of solitude
Is just greater alienation

When I think of you
My life boils over
It happens
Like it's happened many times before
Where are you
I'm floored

When I think of you
I feel guilty just havin' a good time[1]
It's a crime
In what part is all this a creation of mine?

When I think of you…
It's always been cryin' time
Now I see that what's yours
Someone else calls mine

When I think of you…
What I've been unable to share…
Why do I freeze in the moment?
How do I freeze in the moment?
Alone
Alone again
He's always left just standing there

PEOPLE WHO'VE HATED

The stupidity of being unable to side together
All the dinner company was made to feel
   uncomfortable
She ate from the bowl with her fingers
To get at him
To get at *them*
During dessert she rubbed the rum cake into her face
   for fun
Laughing
Daddy went apologizing, chasing after them

People who've hated
For the love of Natasha Kinski
Around here we dress for dignity
Conformity
Decency
And Victoria's secrecy
Gross Vuitton Coquette DeBarge

Ways of a devil
Sleepin' in a lion's den
Some women speak so little
As though in submission
Some go deaf, dumb, and blind

Seeking attention
Attention
Attention

Hatred…
I wrote something about enemies after a war
In the same disco
Workin' it…
Twerkin' it on the floor
Imagine Germans in England
Russians in Poland
Americans in Japan
1944
What's so sad about a sloppy drunk, babbling girl?

Hatred…
Jerry Springer has had a very poor influence
Conflict resolution breaking down
Into unchecked violence
Upright sentient beings
In his palm
A killing floor
I don't know about you
But I've seen a lot of copycat behavior
Greyhound bus patronage
Face-to-face tradin' spit within an inch

Hatred…

They're talkin' pussy and selling ass

On the radio

The adolescent mega-station

Girl power

More power

Today I haven't been berated

Or denigrated

Something's never quite right

Something's always the matter

I go to pieces

And here's another hateful cartoon

For your sweet l'il baby Jesus

SURE AS ANYTHING

Sure as the soul is as hot as the brand
Sure as you'd like to speak with someone
   in command
Sure as that bubbly makes every day the same
Now you're gonna have to find a *new* best friend
   who's game
Sure as anything

Sure as every trend breeds a willing millionaire
In ungodly places y' find ungodliness there
Pressure will make you sit up straight and tall
No discipline seems pleasant at the time, but painful
Sure as anything

Sure as a change of address changes everything and
   nothing at all
Sure as state-sanctioned murder visits the virginal,
   sacrificial doll
Sure as money makes the world go 'round
Love doesn't have any place[2]
Crime pays
Heroes fall
Sure as anything

Sure as jealousy is a very powerful emotion
No answer fits to spring what need be sprung
Sure as there is *something* about your lover that
   defines wicked
The heart it takes to deal with what's already
   been sung
Sure as anything

Sure as you draw a smile
Sure as you can't hide that grin
How can a whole new beginning happen
For one who's only had the carpet pulled out from
   every room he's ever stood in?
Sure as anything

Sure as your daddy was no happy camper
Sure as your mama had to turn her head away
Sure as you were wild, running with the boys
Mercy ain't applied to all spontaneity
No, mercy is *not* applied to all spontaneity

Sure as the status quo is mean upon mean
Sure as a ballad sung from another century
Hey baby, no one suffers like the poor
And what the blood thirsty do so thirst for

Sure as it's awful tempting to sink your teeth in deep
When you bite off more than you can chew y' gotta
   pay the penalty
Sometimes we have the hardest time
Parting with the things we need the least

Sure as a professional must discover a new approach
Sure as it's three minutes to twelve
And Prince Charming's there steppin' out of his
   coach
The fine bones set so exquisitely at each limb's extreme
Immaculate conception
The ossified broach
Sure as square dancing can be such a scream

Praise runs out of praise
Slight gives way to slight, sure enough
Emotions are as physical
As they are merely thoughts
Was it Rimbaud who said, "I've never gotten
   used to it
I've just learned to turn it off?"

Sure as many don't feel complete without
   havoc rampaging

All intended purposes are best met in
    discreet staging

Headhunter
Witch doctor
Pop star
Troubadour
Who do you want to be out there in the *real* world?

Sure as they used to lobotomize people
Cut it out
Burn it shut
End of show
I used to know this tall Indian
He pushed a broom
Oh, here he is now
He's holding a pillow

Sure as phobia is
The child's mind
The superstitious …
"Wanna be in the gang?
Bring us somethin' we can use
No garbage
What belongs to the Lord?
Vengeance

What might be his brand of justice?
Mysterious…
Christ Jesus

Sure as the soul is as hot as the brand
He said, "Don't show up lukewarm
Be red hot or frozen"
I'd walk a thousand miles
Down this road to slip this skin
Yes, I'd walk a thousand miles
Down this road, love
And back again

No Hurry, Soul Creek

It's hard to get smart in a hurry
What we lose for tryin' to keep
It's hard to get smart in a hurry
What we lose for tryin' to keep
It will come back to you
Sometime tomorrow
Or maybe next week
Just as it arrived
In a flurry, so to speak
Soul creek

Everything is sugar and spice
Bumblin' around on the farm
Everything is sugar and spice
Bumblin' around on the farm
It will come back to you
Like another eye, another arm
Just as it arrived
Unabridged and on ice, so to speak
Soul creek

I dropped the heaviest thing on board, Mama
That's all, Mama; that's all

I dropped the heaviest thing on board, Mama
That's all, Mama; that's all
It will come back to you, son
What you were headed toward
Just as it arrived, you'll recall, so to speak
Soul creek

Wind starts t' blowin'
Landslide fallin' down
Wind starts t' blowin'
Landslide fallin' down
It will come back to you
As you've known, so you'll be knowin'
Just as it arrived
Your two feet on the ground
So to speak
Soul creek

INTERPOLATE

I thought of the word 'interpolate' today
I also thought of the words 'reciprocate'
   and 'assimilate'
And another word I don't recall as I went on my way
Can't remember it
Drivin' me crazy
Where was I?
What was that word?
What scene was I in?
What was I thinking?
What was I doing?
'Interpolate' is pretty impressive, though
Interpolate: to read between the lines
Colloquial
Stewing

If you were born to another country
Another society
You'd be enlightened there
And purely patriotic—on *their* side

You may have been nothing but encouraging
To someone who only put you down
Yeah, nothing but encouraging

To someone who doesn't treat you right

On and on

Into oblivion

Got no love in mind

Even space won't make it right

Turn ya into anything they want you to be

Everybody has had a dream where they wake
  up screaming

Medals

Chevrons

Good Samaritans

Outstanding citizens

With their valued opinions

Interpolate

Reciprocate

Assimilate

And that word...

What was it?

Oh ... *abrogate!*

1. repeal or do away with (a law, right, or formal
   agreement).

2. evade (a responsibility or duty).

DEPRESSION

Depression's like somethin' on your shoulders
Y' can't lift up 'n' off your frame
Ask anyone who works two jobs
Day in and day out
He'll tell ya
Them Wall Street boys make enough money
To forget the rest of us ever had names

Depression
Gray
A light fallin' rain
Somethin's been botherin' you a long time
Sometimes you're not sure
If you're the victim or the crime
It's depressing

You're handed something
No dance will carry
No voice so bold
And it came on quick
He ran out and joined the circus
But he don't know how to juggle
Three balls a bit
He don't tell jokes

And he don't laugh at 'em
He don't know any magic tricks
A circus

Depression
Got t' make a new start of it
Got t' see the light
Where you forgive and forget
This has been accomplished
In several instances throughout human history
Though few have heard of it
Forgiveness
What ludicrous is
I and I
In creation where one's nature neither honors
    nor forgives[3]

Depression
Takes your breath away
Steals your outlook
Kills your sense of humor
Affects your will
Your gait
Your drive
Who you now are
Who you once were

Depression's a disease
But the doctors' got no cure
They've done a lot of research on it
But what it is they're still not so sure[4]

Depression is a national characteristic
And it has been for a long time
Don't kid yourself
Depression leads to homicide and suicide
The wasteland of the mind
Modern times
(Seth Meyers, roll on!)

Depression
I told my doctor everything
He told me, "Come back next week
We need to talk some more"
And over a period of months
We got to know each other better
He explained to me
These pills are not a cure
They only help you to think a little better
A little straighter
A little longer
Neurochemical balancers
An equalizer to an amplifier

The treble and bass
The mids the highs the lows
On the dials of your receiver
Getting the picture?
Your quality of life can improve
If you eat 'em twice a day with food

Depression
But mostly…
Depression is something y' must outrun
How's that done?
What is "depressed?"
Am *I* depressed?
Is this the road to Nazareth?

Depression
Cocaine and alcohol
And more cocaine and alcohol
The eventual outcome
Is like all things eventual
Cocaine and alcohol
We're self-medicating right tonight, aren't we y'all?

Depression
Doctor Dolittle's secretary, Nancy Haarüt

Carried in her purse

This thing she liked to toot

Gave him a taste one day…

And *Dude!*

He bought a hot air balloon

And everything was beautiful in its own way

Depression

LOUISIANA BUST

I've got a few stacks of papers to get lost in
Other men use a jackhammer at work
Sittin' in the sun on the Mississippi River
Chicory
Spiced tea
A real friendly stranger with a real friendly perk

Maybe I'll bring some "decent"
Of course I'll bring some
All I need is a Louisiana bust
Got no friend there
None
But I know I'm lookin' for one
Anyways … cocaine …
You never need to carry much

Halloween
Drumstick
Fluorescent green
Ghostly gray against white body paint
If you can blend into the scene
On Halloween in New Orleans
You just might live to see the feathers of the
    Mardi Gras Saint

New Orleans loves a parade
Moonshine visions
Staggering chicks on too-high heels with
   tearstained cheeks
You've got to go deeper in
You got to roam
To hear the cloppedy-clop of the Quarter's
   cobblestone
There's a sight
Looks like a playwright
"Baby you go mess with him
I'll go hide in the closet at home"

Will I straighten up this two-room apartment?
Pack my bags and order tickets?
Goin' to the old Gulf Coast's river city
Thirty years ago I sat in that rooftop window
In need of a touch of tenderness
Even a sister's pity

The blackbirds in the churchyard
Must 've had a fitful night
Cawing on the down-low
Before dawn's first light
What does that sound like?
Like nothin' else…

Sounds like they'd like to damn God himself

The birdbath

The Yip shop

Black gates of iron lattice

Way back in the Quarter past dark

They're sweated

Watching themselves gavotte

Leather and lace

Twisted into a knot

A young tap-dancer

Makin' it spark

Torch-lit streets that wind around and around

Till they disappear into a spot

They say the whole place is haunted

By the ghosts of slaves who knew the auction block

A bayou is an endless swamp

Only black umbrellas at the souvenir shop

"Something special, sir?"

"Yes, something … *special*"

"Well, sir…

Across the bridge there's a cheeky little joint

In the attic of a Bahá'í temple

You're greeted at the door

The rest is very simple

But sir…
I hear the real money is with our best-kept secret
It's called the Heart-shaped Hideaway
Sixteen windows
A woman's face in every frame
There are chambers along this very street
Where people line up to lose their inhibitions…
Where people wear masks
So no one might know their names"

I for one have no wish to go back down there
Its memories to me are just too much to bear
I don't need a reminder of what was always too
    much to see
Anyway, who the hell wants to go drinkin' on
    Bourbon Street?
College boys from LSU
Each with futures in fine Italian shoes
Hey, where you fellas from?

Trombone Shorty and all the heavy hitters
Can be found on Tuesdays at Preservation Hall

Dat ol' dry stuff…
If you wan' t' die o' jazz pois'nin'
Vodka's all…

New Orleans' got the infirmary
But they're still waitin' for the ambulance to come
And if only they could keep the window screens on
Humming birds buzz 'round the porches of the
   old plantations

   Who Dat?"
   Oh, Shorty! What you got?
   Shoo…
   Man, let's burn one

It's called a "Rusty Nail" in Shreveport
Here it's called a "Hurricane"
New Orleans …
It's the smallest town with the biggest name
Somewhere along this street
Anne Rice is having another Jim Beam

If I go …
All I'll get is a good look
At the cracks in the sidewalk of Jackson Square
There is no clown so fine
As the one who *ruled* when I was there
I've no need *whatsoever*
To stand in the spot where I picked a mandolin
An escalator

A fudge shop
I didn't have to wear a hat
But I was glad to have the pin

If you don't have a place to stay in the Big Easy, Jack
You're walkin' with po' boys who do more than
　　pick pockets
They prey in packs
No one's got your back
Oh, please … please don't take my locket

Pretty lady gets exclusive invite to the rooftop star-
　　light bars in the city
You're invited but your friend can't come
Strictly VIP
It's not at all "kid friendly"
In fact, it's old 42nd Street in NYC
The name of the game is "Love Your Money"
Are you being extorted
Or have you now chosen to live this life, honey?

There was a porn theater
Playing a movie called *Cat House Fever*
I stood in front by the marquee and looked at
　　the poster
Must 've been closed…

I didn't go in...
I'd remember
I knew a girl at Tulane studying architecture
The days turned into weeks
In a few months it was all over
I saw her facing away from the mirror in the parlor
And then and there I knew what it was
To feel like a loser

What month are we in?
It's the one that turns frosty cold
Better pack a jacket
My scarf
Some gloves
The radio
Really, I know I'm strung a little too tight for
    that city
But I'm sure gonna eat me some St. Charles Tavern
    brown crawfish gumbo
You shouldn't be alone in New Orleans
No, in New Orleans you shouldn't be alone

If I want New Orleans
I can find some band blowin' triplets in any
    music hall
I can hold the hand of Randy Newman's babysitter

Just like you, I've tried it all…
A time or two
Yeah, tried that, too

The preservation society sniffs out anything
   too smooth
If I want New Orleans, I can pick up and go today
If I want New Orleans…

Jock-a-mo fee-no ai na-né
Jock-a-mo fee na-né
Talk-in' 'bout, hey now!
Hey now!
Iko, Iko, un-day
Jock-a-mo fee-no ai na-né
Jock-a-mo fee na-n[5]

I can tell you all about that Shreveport drummer
He came one winter
Was in Nashville by summer
Tell us all about your first kiss, sailor
Tell us about *The River Queen*
Tell us about the way the people moved …
What they clung fast to…
Or seemed loath to convene
Chicory … chicory and pralines

Went down there
Felt the world sink
The mother lode
I ain't goin' back down there
Til I can afford a house on Garden District Road
Fog banks and river bridges
Grafitti and tourists
Drunks on binges

It's sinkin'…
It's sinkin'
You can feel the ground sinkin'

A man seated there wearing a long black coat
I went and sat down next to him
Read him some stuff I'd wrote

Show me a hero
I'll show you a tragedy
That's F. Scott Fitzgerald Kennedy
You meant so much to me
You wouldn't have done to me what you did to me
If you knew what you did to me had done to me

A lot of good it did ya
New Orleans, farewell I bid ya

Somethin's stuck in my throat
I know you've got your lines memorized
I, too, have a few by rote

PO BOY ALLEY BLUES

Spinning top
Matchbox dock
Is every thief a crook?
Spinning top
Matchbox dock
Is every thief a crook?
Life
Don't it serve up enough
To make Fyodor Dostoyevsky look?

To greet the dawn
No one around
Moonset sanctified spice
The purple dawn
No one around
Moonset sanctified spice
This seaside row of houses is owned by people
Who I'm sure are very nice

I run the tape back in my mind
My pulse begins to hammer away
I run the tape back in my mind
My pulse begins to hammer away
I feel something akin to a deal goin' down

She can do wondrous works with your fate

I don't have any baseball cap from Newfoundland
I don't have a tee-shirt from Nova Scotia
I don't have any baseball cap from Newfoundland
I don't have a tee-shirt from Nova Scotia
The nature of man is to beg and to steal
To lie and deceive
You can go tell him I told ya

LADY GREYHOUND'S WINDOW

Another man's yard
Another man's tree
The brambles
The briars
The buckeyes
The leaves

Wouldn't want to go through that again
Wouldn't want to go through that twice
Can't get far enough away from the farm
Or the city streets' blinding ice

Ok, makes sense
No such thing as mistakes
Whatever might've been from whatever once was
I was supposed to love her cousin
And then become irrevocably hers
But love spit love
Whatever once was
Irrevocably hers
Love spit love

In the land of milk and honey
The kind of milk and honey from the tropic of guns
    and money

Walking alone
Come some young soldiers in a jeep
Something happened to me there
In that village where I took my sleep
Like a journey through dark heat[6]
The corral
The horses
The sun
The dust
Let me up; I've had enough![7]

The awesome fact of a big black cargo ship
And at just forty yards, headin' out
Free of its slip
Good clip
She said, "You're a lonesome fellow; I can tell it"
Sittin' here writing in this inlet
Come tell me your story
Let's go have coffee in an alley off the strip

Little bird
Come whisper in my ear
To live above the law you must be honest
Not only is there a blacklist
There's a blacklist of blacklists

Little bird
Little pest

Big lazy river
Well of a spring
Pools in a delta
Tides changing
Furious
The rapids at the bottom of the canyon
Time marches on in its own abandon

What's that leather thing hippy chicks wear in their
    hair?
Oh right, a barrette
Hand pressed and painted
Cuff and spear
You'll find me in the market with a full basket in the
    evening
I'll be selling there
This one would look good in your thick, brown hair

To feel the earth move under my feet
Tumblin' down with love in the air
An unexpected kiss by the light on the street
Come knock me down, sugar bear

Whatever became of that fortress?
That stone-cut palace by the sea?
In a room next door two lovers, *amor*
One of 'em had the same first name as me

Plain in her ways
Simple in taste
Of little need
The caged bird ends up in the cat's mouth
Right about the time it's freed

Why don't you step back and use those magic
   powers
To find out what kind of feelings I've got?
Tell me what it was you said you'd be proud to have
Tell me
Once sewn
Once sought

HOLY SMOKES

Holy smokes
I got 18 eyes
I got 18 eyes
Take a look
Holy smokes
I got 18 eyes
I got 18 eyes
Hand on the book!

One eye got somethin' stuck up under the lid
One only sees in black and white, kid
One I wanna rub so bad, there must be a sty…
I use a lot o' Visine
Who's ok to drive?

Two eyes read the paper
Cover to cover
Yeah, two never tire of watching
Lady Chatterly's Lover
These two down here got something cooking
These two are so tired
Their eyelids are drooping

These two sting
Like they've been hit by mace
Friend, these two here feel like they're fallin' out o'
   my fuckin' face
Can't get up off the couch
I live for TV
I lost the remote last week
You don't know what it did to me

When these two eyes close
Mysteriously, I begin to sing
When these two eyes swell with tears
I hear Gregorian chanting

This one here is dilated
Been that way since one day when...
It had never been that orange before
RFK Stadium, Washington 1986
Which was somewhere right around '87

Look
This one is doing something ever so meticulously
And this one seems to be lost in a dream
This one is writing cute poetry
Begging the question
"What's to become of me?"

One's looking down on my two feet in the mud

This one is waiting for a chariot of God

Two are big and brown

Two are icy blue

Two belong to a cynic

Always knowing just what's wrong with you

Don't stand so close to the screen, son

It's not good for you

These two just can't put down a good book

And these two are still nauseated from the ferry ride
  they took

These two got a job at the sunglass boutique

Standing there in ovals

Aviators

And other styles of the classic, antique

These two were on a list

Donated by a motorcyclist

He came from Illinois

I'm holding them here

For someone else to own

And bless

And enjoy

Two eyes on the door
Two stare at the wall
One looks pretty bored
This pair can clearly see through it *all*

Do they all blink together
Together in unison?
Yes
They all blink together in unison, I think
All kinds of stuff starts happenin'
When one of 'em gets wise to a wink

This one is squinting from the light of the sun
This one looks like he could be aiming a gun
This one really likes James Bond
This one's staring off beyond the horizon

Is that 18?
18 eyes or something in between?
Now, where did I put my glasses?
Has anyone seen my keys?

Some dreams are too damn strange
Some dreams are too damn real

Cross two strange with two real

A few too many times

Your point of view

May become, shall we say, "surreal?"

Holy smokes

I got 18 eyes

I got 18 eyes

Take a look

Holy smokes

I got 18 eyes

I got 18 eyes

Leaves y' shook!

HEY BLACK GIRL

Hey black girl
I can't run my hands through your hair
Hey black girl
You get a stiff neck when I pull you near

No disrespect, girl
But y' head's all wet 'n' greasy
Don't get me wrong, girl
Let's talk about natural beauty
Nice-n-easy, now
Nice-n-easy

I know it's shallow, black girl
I know its only skin deep
But it is you, black girl, who must understand
Dread is what you're born with
And dread is what y' keep

Y' been livin' on candy and chips
And juice from the corner store, black girl
You been stroking faux feathers with false fingernails
'n' those fake eyelashes, in Jheri Curls

On the TV, black girl
Your people been depicted as clowns
Is it any wonder that you can't seem to settle down?

Black lady, black girl
On our first date I wore my favorite flannel shirt
And my best blue jeans
You were all done up like a homecoming queen

Dark queen
These sorority sisters
For me, they'll never do
Ebony, the color of evening
You are that love to me
Woman, I have no reservations about saying
How much and how deeply I feel for you
I'm in love with a black woman
And I'm so glad

Cindy and Jenny and Dorothy and Liz
I'm not even moved to try
One may be prettier than the next
But to kiss you, black girl…
To kiss you is to kiss every star in the sky

Black lady, black girl
You are so beautiful to me
This world's on its side like a fallen tree
To stand by your side
Proudly
I and I, black girl
Come take ahold of me

It matters to me where you're goin'
It matters to me where you've been
I love it when we're out walkin'
And I love to get you talkin'
I know your heart has known a greater sufferin'

Eyes of an angel
Teeth like pearl
Lips made to kiss
You're my only love, black girl
Before you, I roamed the world
In my own bitterness
Before you were known to me
I didn't know I could feel like this

Black lady, black girl
So much comes down the line that just ain't
   happenin'

Where nothing rings true
The differences we carry could keep everything
   fresh
Tan like me
Brown like you

Black lady
In another lifetime y' must've owned the world
I just can't help but put you up on a pedestal
The two of us
Companions
Ever respectful

Black lady, black girl
Tell me what you'd like to do
Tell me where you'd like to go
Imagine us together as lovers forever
You've got so much I don't know
My soul, black lady
My soul…
Black lady, black girl

ALWAYS ALONE

I am always alone
Oh lord its true
And all I've got is this paper and pen to get even
Am I shunted?
Do I do as the shunted do?

I am always alone
Like an alabaster statue
Like a playwright whose writin' days are pretty
   much through
It gets old
Broken love
And endless despair
And who wants to hear you bitch and moan?
No one
No one anywhere

Always alone
What a waste of life
I've got to find a way to stop playing this role
To turn the page
To gain a partner
Two halves make a whole

Well, I'm always alone
It's some kind of pain
A holy man would cock his head and ask
"What's working against itself, here?
What are you trying to gain?"

I'm forced now to be with this man who's
    always alone
He don't wanna swim
He don't want to walk
He don't ride
These things, these activities y' do solo
Alone
Got a light?

Movin' on has proved impossible
Movin on
Learning to lose
Joy is a malady
Right, a guitar
I'm just another white boy singin' the blues

Alone, nothin crosses over
I'd buy me a few hours with a lady of the night
Don't know why I don't
I'm conflicted

I'm broken

Full of regret

Sadness

Don't know why I don't

Escort

L.A. snort

Alone, always alone

This gown I've found

This self-imposed jail

This ... this tree losin' its leaves

Doin time is doin time

Ain't I done mine?

One day Ol' Billy Delions

He started to grieve

I build it up and build it up until it's solid

Solid as a rock

And then I get so ... I can't think straight

I meet myself

I'm genuinely distraught

God don't care about a million bucks

God don't care about things that don't mean

   that much

Alone

Pat myself on the back
One hand clapping
Nevertheless…
To live absent of touch or caress
Is to live impoverished
To face yourself
Are you that serious?

Alone
Can't sit back and wait for things to come to you
Y' got to go out and get 'em!
All the lonely people
Where do they all came from
All the lonely people
Where do they all belong?[8]

MOMENTS THAT I LOVE YOU

There's a moment that I love you
When you're tired
And your eyes are so blue

There's a moment that I love you
There's a glow
Your face has its own light shining through

There's a moment that I love you
When your hair gets that sheen
Like that day on the beach with Mare Stella in
    Old St. Augustine

There's a moment when I love you
When your whole voice fills the space
And everything about you is like a circumstance of
    grace

These moments that I love you
What we had was dear
These moments …
I'm drawn to pull somebody near

Moments that teach me
To be taught
Moments that catch me
To be caught
Moments that raise me
To rise
We never fought did we, you and I?

These moments that I love you
I guess there always will be
These moments that I love you
I cannot let them kill me

And these moments that I love you
They've been there before
I've been running away from it for so long
Runnin' not to feel it anymore

These moments that I love you
These moments that I love you

RAINDROPS ON A TIN CAN

I don't need to sit around endlessly wondering
About what spending time with you would be like…
Brown eyed-girls with broken noses
Is just a body type
Would've done me a world of good
To try to believe that years ago
How many years?
I'm sorry…
That's not a place I really like to go

Raindrops on a tin can
You've given those men the keys to the kingdom
Palms of the arc
A treasure chest
You're a woman of the world now, Madam
I can't hold it against 'ya
If I wasn't your man
I'd prob'bly be celebratory
Astonished
Most decidedly impressed
Oh, sister
How thou art truly blessed

Raindrops on a tin can

What once hurt

What I was sorry for

How many days died the same?

No, really…

For once…

How many days died the same?

Kept turning out

And burning out

And turning out the same

Put two gold stars next to my name

I have an apology

But you've already tipped the scales

Evening the score

It's said that your mother tongue is a language
   of intolerance

To think we're this tangled up

Having shared the same heritage

Evening the score…

What did he once *have to* give someone up for?

Raindrops on a tin can

Satisfaction

We find it or we find it not

Funny thing

At the end of *Social Network*

Barbie's tail feather was tamale red

Fuchsia hot

I've never suffered your voice or your face

Your eyes or your body

In sexually charged dreams

In this way I'm sure the Lord has shown me mercy

Spared me

Satisfied?

Dripping

I need three medications twice a day

To keep me from bottoming out

I've turned into one of those people

Who's forever working things out

They say that woman is the weaker sex

You can bet she overcompensates

And her loyalty is as quixotic as her mood

Now *that* is an overstatement

Her mood…

The tides

The rain

The moon

Raindrops on a tin can

This is where teardrops fall

Far away and over the wall

And time

Time

The time begins to crawl

Suddenly … glacial

I thought I heard a young man cryin' this morning

Primal

Final

Yes, I heard someone cryin' this morning

TO HAVE YOURSELF TO BLAME

To have yourself to blame
What's in there you need to forgive in order to forget?
To have it
To hold it
To deal with what shame?
To get over it
Once you have yourself to blame

Every man got to make his share of mistakes
Just to land and stand himself up
That there tree is a lemon tree
With some sugar and some ice
We can drink it right up

The hardest thing to do is to live with yourself
They don't tell you that the day you're born
I feel so bad I could beat my dog
Smoke enough cigarettes to see my health take a turn

Tell me that isn't true
Y' been seen around town holdin' someone else's
    hand
Where y' been don't bother me

Oh, please…
What's the use to pretend?

To suffer loss of heart
Right where there was some place to start
I want to strike out in the worst of ways
Lie down and die
Run out in the dark

I'd rather be in some dark hollow
Where the sun don't ever shine
Between love and hate
I, for one, have had quite a time

All at once the world becomes an empty place
Profoundly empty
A haunted house
Aquarius drinks juice in the kitchen
Capricorn's lost in the basement
Cancer holds the cat that ate the mouse

How we danced the night away
Changing partners
Waltzing the floor
We played duck-duck-goose in the parlor
Told nursery rhymes 'til dawn in the old orchard

What was I thinkin' this morning?
Something 'bout her suitors comin' to call
An anklet of Hawkmoon shale from him
Leon brought a signed Chagall

And who was lying in wait
A lowly devil or a lofty god?
There are a whole lot of rooms in Buckingham Palace
   to get lost in
Old boy games in the backyard

What am I hung up over?
Did someone do somebody wrong?
It's called a "dirge" when everybody bites the dust
A dirge is another kind of song

For as long as north goes east
And west stays where west is…
It's the tip of the whip that strikes the flesh
Under arrest is what under arrest is

That's the legendary white knight
That's the feral peasant child
Fair packed up
Took a chest full of loot
That'd leave any tyrant beguiled

Talk about self-respect

Here's Prince Machiavelli

Who have *you* ever been caught washing your
  hands with

Here at this basin of modernity?

Dusty broom in the corner

Raggedy mop on the floor

Whatever it is I came here to get away from

It's a shame…

I don't remember anymore

If I leap from this tree so deep in the woods

Will she dream of me tonight?

Oh, no, no

I've been through this movie before

When it's over, you just never feel quite right

To have yourself to blame

To know how it feels to stand all night in the
  pourin' rain

How else to wash some memories from the brain?[9]

The spirit…

Does it know your voice

Your face

Your name?

To have yourself to blame

What's in there you need to forgive in order to forget?

To have it

To hold it

To deal with what shame?

To get over it

Once you have yourself to blame

ALL OF GOD'S MERCY

In all of God's mercy
Would you find a place?
What flowers of indulgence?
What kind of vase?
Lord, Lord
Would you find a place?

In all of God's mercy
Would you find a place?
Many go to run
Who wouldn't run the race
Lord, lord
Would you find a place?

But for the grace of God
There goes I…
I heard somebody talking a particular way
But for the grace of God
There goes I…
I heard somebody talking
And I had something to say

In all of God's mercy
Would you find a place?

What of confidence?
Our sins?
Our secrets?
Leather and lace
Belladonna
Would you find a place?

But for the grace of God
There goes I...
Mercy, mercy me
But for the grace of God
There goes I...
What can I do for thee?

In all of God's mercy
Would you find a place?
Wherever you are welcome
Is where you will be
Makes sense
The sense it makes
Lord, lord
Would you find a place?

You Said "I Love Love"

"Oh, you said I love love…"
And water is wet
And grass is green
And cold bites
And smoke is slick
And girls are cats
And boys clog
And one day we're reassigned
By administrating angels of God

And airplanes float
And boats heel
And lizards sun
And orders land
And harvest moons
And master strokes
And thunderous drums
And inalienable rights
And slander remains
And crossword puzzles
And chicken soup
And the ground is moving
And psychosomatic illness is all that there is
And you said "you love love"

Doesn't that jus' say it all?

May your aim be true

THE BLACK ARTS

The black arts
Are where God and the devil go tinkering
They find each other's company to be
   most repugnant
Sickening

The black arts
Read it twice
The directions
Warnings signs
No one can protect you from it
Once y' turn it on
Sign right there on the dotted line

The black arts
The other side of the exception to the rule
Of course you loved to watch *Quantum Leap*
Quantum Leap is *Matrix* cool

Everywhere you go
There's always someone ready
To take you to school
You've given him real American dollar bills
To have been made a fool by a fool

The black arts
Wanna buy a watch, friend?
What does the devil need?
Devil needs time
Beetle Juice, Beetle Juice, Beetle Juice
No butts: back of the line

The black arts
Thicker than blood
Blacker than ink
The more you struggle the quicker you sink
Artists so tortured
Rebels so plagued
Boss, it's ninety-six degrees in the shade

Good intentions can be evil
Both hands can be full of grease
Could be standing next to you
The person you notice least

You cannot depend on it to be your guide
When it's you who must keep it satisfied
Delusions of grandeur
An evil eye
Gives you the idea
You're too good to die

Crowd behavior
Group mentality
I and I
I and I

How many hours are there in a seven-day week?
Is it divisible by two?
How about three?
Neat
Have a seat

All of them hold strong delusion
All are ministers of the trade
How much did you do?
And then you did *what?*
Weren't you at all afraid?
She loved most hangin' with the guys…
When power took the place of where love lies

Witchcraft scum
Exploiting the dumb
Turnin' children into punks and slaves
Whose heroes and healers are rich dope dealers
Who should be put in their graves
(Tell the truth, now)[10]

A man in a long black coat
Oh, they'll push your buttons
They'll get your goat
I'd rather be in some dark hollow
Where the sun don't ever shine
Than know you're another man's darlin'
Why is it to me still such a crime?
Oh, Mexico
Gone to stay this time

The black arts
The first thunderstorms of the season
Might tempt you to go walkin' without reason
Between the devil and the deep blue sea
Time stands still
You and God
No, God and me

CHANGE YOUR ART AROUND

Change your art around once in a while
Your furniture
Your flat
Your room
Your yard
You know how good you feel when you clean out
   your car

You learn to write your name
You learn to tie your shoes
You learn to hold a fork and knife
You learn to set the needle
Not to scratch the vinyl…
Boy!
The vinyl between the grooves

These things you know better than me
Naturally
Well, you know 'em so well
All those jolly men took a knee
Sayin', "Please Miss Mousy
Won't you marry me?"

How did all this happen?

Tell me

I've got to know!

I need to know!

Maiche…

It blew up like a bomb

Metastasized like a tumor

Like a bare-assed Hollywood rumor

I love you so much I *hate* you, Maiche

Tell me…

I've got to know

REN

Ren
You are a thousand campfires
Maybe more
Your mother's love of Albert Einstein
Wheatgrass and treehouses
Your daughter, Savannah, holding a baby raccoon
Little Jeremiah following her around
The rope in the tree you pulled
That made the rainwater fall from above
Your beat-up pickup truck
What I remember of you
I very much like to be reminded of
You are the gold of our people
Its time
Its endurance
Its lit, canvas tents
I could so get lost in that…
In you…
Ren

—Maiche

ORTHODOXY

People come to adopt

Some form of orthodoxy in their lives

As dust gathers

And needs to be swept

Regularly

WHEN GOD SAYS…

When God says y' should 've known better
Not another syllable's heard
He already told ya "I won't tell ya again"
He's got a way of lettin' ya know y' been served

When God has had enough
You'll feel the ground rumble
It ain't a dream no more
He's on to ya
Trouble…
Trouble…
Trouble…
Nothin' but trouble

God don't play patty-cakes forever
Only love a woman in your comfort zone
That's the eleventh commandment
It just didn't fit there at the bottom of the stone

When God says y' should 've known better
There'll be no more of this baby talk
When God says y' should 've known better
That's the last straw…
The final cut

SEARCH ME OUT

Oh, when I say search me out
Gonna be some bells ringing out
When I say search me out
Some bells gonna ring long and solemn
There'll be chimes and pipes and drums about
Samson's columns
Search me out

When I come to say, "Search me out"
What will you find in my heart?
When I come to say, "Search me out"
Of what did I allow myself to become a part?

Search me
Search me out
House made of straw
House made of wood
House made of brick
The windows all broken
Newspapers stacked
The overgrowth's thick
Does anybody really live in it?

Search me

Search me out

Better not cry

Better not pout

I must be guilty of something

Come whisper it into my ear

Tell me what it's all about, Punkin

Yes, search me

Search me out

What do I want and why do I want it?

Who am I, anyway?

To feel about something tomorrow

The same way you felt about it today

Search me

Search me out

What manifests in the mind of constant disdain?

Somebody made a million bucks on foam rubber
   rocks

To throw at the goddamned thing

Search me

Search me out

Am I likely to digest reflection on my own?

No…

Search me

Search me out

Oh where, oh where did all the snakes in Ireland go?

Search me

Search me out

What have I got?

I've got my feet in two worlds, maybe three

What kind of a friend or citizen?

He just walks down the street with one hand waving
  free

Here he comes again

Somehow I've been searched out

These are the chains and the rags I wear

   Tree fell on me

   Bust'd my arm

   No one come

   Boss don't care

Mr. Kansas City Candyman

Funky Struttin' Boogie Two Shoes

He ain't all there, is he?

Nah, he ain't at *all* all there
That's a walkin' talkin' man tryin' to shake his
blues, Izzy

Search me
Search me out

LADYFINGER ELEGANT

Joyce
Something about you is fragile, delicate
Something about you is elegant…
Ladyfinger elegant
The boys gotta stand back and show respect
See 'em in their uneasy etiquette?
Something there is about you…
I'm just so crazy about it

Joyce
Your nametag says 'Mallory' but I see a 'Joyce'
You've got a baby face and a low, clear voice
Full-time in that pharmacy
Is a rebel's last stand
I walk through
Feelin' kinda creepy
Forty-something
Aisle three
Burt's Bees
Dirty old man

Joyce
Let's do lunch sometime, maybe

Drum circle
First Thursdays on eighteenth, off the abbey
And if we become friends
Days off or Sundays
I'm bound to breach your personal space
B' b' b' babyface

Joyce
Aren't you so easy on the eyes?
I could give you a squeeze
"Child, please"
Spin you like a top
Make the world stop
You really do take my breath away from me, Joyce

Be leary of a man who puts you on a pedestal
Or a man who comes bearing gifts
Have you ever been to New Orleans in April?
Jazz fest
Sun hat
Sun dress
Po-boy sandwich

Girl, I'd be happy to go to a football game
But you know I'd rather park it by the river

The sun so invitingly warm

Each wave of laughter

Each qu-iiiii-v-v-v-ver-r-r-r-r

Joyce

What's it like to have someone chasing after you?

Romancing the stone?

Woman we'd be having a better conversation

If I could step right through this here telephone

Joyce

For you

One of those monstrous bottles of French perfume

To keep you properly occupied

I'd have to rob a bank or two

And soon!

I've got to teach you how they dance in Jamaica

You gonna git to feelin' betta, sistah!

Let's just go somewhere together

Me 'n' you

Got someone better?

Joyce…

I mean Mallory…

I mean Joyce

I haven't even mentioned your curls
So full, so dark
I know you can't stand it that you're really
a girly-girl

One day I looked up from kneeling by
the magazines
Saw two big, electric, navy blue eyes
And I saw you once at 10:00pm when the
grind begins
They'd turned green
Green like southern fireflies

Joyce
I'll write you a song
Paint you a picture
Move next door
Hack all your fixtures
You'll open your windows to drums and guitars
When the moon is full
I'll put funny things on your car

Joyce
You must be this town's good luck charm
You could take New York City

"Stacey's mom has got it goin' on"
"Stacey's mom has got it goin' on"
Like in the movie, *Down and Out in Beverly Hills*
The older sister
A little funny
A little googly
Joyce, that's how you're pretty

Something about you that is fragile, delicate
Something about you is elegant …
Ladyfinger elegant
The young girl knows what the old man wants…
How many years do you get for bank robbery 'round
    these parts?
Something there is about you
Maybe we fit?
"Easy now boy, easy"
Ladyfinger elegant…

'BOUT TO GIVE WAY

How long have I been this way?
Doesn't even have a name
I know too well what come tomorrow
Tomorrow come another day
Is it too late for me to learn how to pray?
Slippery stones in my pathway
'Bout to give way

How long have I been this way?
Doesn't even have a name
I know too well what come tomorrow
Tomorrow come another day
Of this my heart sickened
Of this I complain
Slippery stones in my pathway
'Bout to give way

It's a few years now since I opened this drawer
This drawer I keep my mind in…
This number stapled right here … is stellar
This one with coffee stains is just right
'Cept the end needs somethin' to tie it all back to the
    beginning

How long have I been this way?

Doesn't even have a name

I know too well what come tomorrow

Tomorrow come another day

Become someone to another

Or you'll freeze up

And shatter

And just blow away

Slippery stones in my pathway

'Bout to give way

How long, oh, how long have I been this way?

Doesn't even have a name

I know too well what come tomorrow

Tomorrow come another day

I guess being satisfied is just having no one left
   to blame[11]

How 'bout it…?

Me and you, babe

Slippery stones in my pathway

'Bout to give way

Oh, well…

A touch of gray

Kinda suits ya anyway

And that was all I had to say

And…

Slippery stones in my pathway

'Bout to give way

Slippery stones in my pathway

'Bout to give way

BLOOD LAW

Blood law

News from the hospital

Blood law

Shock and awe

Lord, Lord

Sudden death

Lord, Lord

I will dance ever upward after I take my last breath

One's day's final

Blood law

Shekels

All through the bible

One and all

Blood law

Libel

Blood law

Destiny manifest

Yes, yes...

Tell us about being truly blessed

God must be the original lunatic

Quick, look up "psychosomatic"

You mean we can make ourselves sick?

Blood law

Main Street draw

Blood law

En garde!

Blood law

Get off my lawn!

Blood law

Thirty: love

Blood law

Grin and bear it

Yeah, yeah…

Be patient

Keep a stiff upper lip

He and his friends

Will make themselves hated

Got something to share?

Don't be too quick to share it

Unless you do, don't laugh out loud

Now showing:

What in this world you are most and least proud of

Blood law

There's always one in every crowd

Blood law

Wrecking ball

Godlessly irresponsible

Spontaneously corruptible

Girl power

More power

Barbie

Jello

Jack Daniels

Not that you're not a fantastically conglomerated
   intellectual

And otherwise quite a remarkable individual

Blood law

A musical

Blind ambition

Insatiable greed

Perversion is what happens to other people

Clive Davis killed Whitney Houston

With a playlist no one could believe

Blood law

Those California kids

Burn it at both ends

Those California kids

Throw the whole damned thing in

Blood law

Proving grounds

Shooting galleries

Sinbad sat on the shore for a season
Before he sailed the seven seas
A little something before the show?
Strange behaviour at the Guggenheim museum
Are you my mother?
Go dog, go!
Jackson Pollock
Leroy Neiman

Blood law
Don't look back, Lot
Your wife has turned to salt
Don't look back, Lot
It must be partially your fault
When Johnny comes marching home
When Johnny strikes up the band
Johnny come lately
You're too bad, Johnny
Johnny, you're too bad
You're too bad, Johnny
Johnny, you're too bad

Blood law
Don't bear false witness
God don't forgive this
Nor does he suffer much cognitive dissonance

Slow to anger, God is

Hopeful, faithful

Long on patience

Blood law

That is murder

That is cruelty

That is an epidemic that killed hundreds of
    millions globally

My God!

That is circumcising femininity

Bestiality

Uncleanliness

Incest

Jealousy

Envy

Things commanded of thee

A conscience … unto death

Reputation above all

They say the rest is commentary

Blood law is the inevitabilities

Blood law

Let's Make a Deal

The Price is Right

Jeopardy

The Wheel of Fortune

In one single note I can name that tune
Jack in the Box
The inspired on FOX
National Public Radio
Where fund drives are few
And commercials are not
Good morning, Mr. Koch…
And good morning, Mr. Koch

Blood law
Exposure to the sun
Parts per million
You make the most unbelievable pancakes, hon
A play on words
A living will
The stain on the marble steps
Of the capital

Blood law
Biorythmic status
Abacab is anywhere there has been an abacus
Abacab is *anywhere* there *is* an abacus
When there is no moon in the month of May
June, July, August…
Keep myself in a dialogue

So much to discuss
Too-rah loo-rah too-rah loo-rah yay
Running through the veins
Thick like oil
Blacker than ink

Blood law
Mercy
Forgiveness
Respect
Loving kindness
The church of the heart of the poisonous

Blood law
Presently
Blood law
Destiny
Blood law
D' Dog an' d' Cat

D' dog luv d' cat
D' dog luv d' cat *whole!*

But d' dog don' luv d' cat
When d' cat eatin' out d' dog's bowl!

REHAB REC ROOM
BATHROOM TALK

It used to be I'd think of thee
Very frequently
After that it was just once in a while
It used to be I'd think of thee
Very frequently
After that it was just once in a while
I don't need nothin' tonight, no
Azucar, half-n-half, *café Americano*

I just can't put myself through it tonight
But the night is young, y' never know
I just can't put myself through it tonight
But the night is young, y'never know
I don't need nothin' tonight, no
Only your good company
Some ginger and soy, wasabi, masago

My heart is not heavy
It's light and it's free
But, sometimes my burden is more than I can bear
My heart is not heavy
It's light and it's free
But, sometimes my burden is more than I can bear

I don't need nothin' tonight, no
No ... well maybe some o' that Café Bustelo?

I need to walk all night
Till the broad daylight
My dog, my pack, some water
Yes ... I'm gonna walk all night
Till the broad daylight
Take a break
Smoke me a saucer
I don't need a thing tonight ... no
"Hey, Maiche, Whatcha doin' tonight?
Y' home?
Got any dough?"

REUNION

Mrs. Hillman was an old softie

Ms. Kaminester smiled so pretty, didn't she?

Mrs. Kerns wasn't Beyonce

She was Donna Summers

Back in the day

I liked being right on top in her class

And that year seemed to have gone by so fast

Mr. Carol was proud and gay

That was the fourth grade

He'd talk of his travels for half the day

If you asked the right way

Mrs. Bearman was hunchbacked and blonde

She looked a little like Tom Petty

And her voice — so nasal

I don't know … It may have turned me on

Mr. Boyle came from Beantown

He had a green spitfire — British Leyland

Best teacher to be found

Blue-eyed, direct, and laughing

Mrs. Feller smoked

Mrs. Carillon joked

Mr. Greenhut was a prison guard

Mrs. Gary's big hair taught art

Mr. Zelesky's composer walls

Mr. Frank mopped up the halls

Mr. Farnsworth taught math

In Mrs. Taylor's English class there were sentences
   to graph

I swear—in ten months, not once did this woman
   laugh

Mr. Miller was a true friend

Kuchalakas ("Kuch," remember him?)

"What's that…?

Another lap for you, Mr. Charlie Chickenlooper!"

Mr. Bloomstein

God rest his soul

¿Susana *está en casa?*

¿Susana está en casa?

¿Susana está en casa?

¿Susana está en casa?

¡Yo!

My buddy Sean was no go on the *accénto*

Mr. Kesselman became a principal

Got himself into a little trouble

I don't remember much about the 9th grade

I was all braided up in puppy love braids

Afghani Danny took our allowance money

Being president of CSI wasn't all that funny

I don't remember Ms. Comeau

I do remember Coach Hayes
I remember Coach Kunst
He worked out with the Celtics
Told me about it once
And good old Coach Aquino
He taught sex-ed and turned red as a tomato
Little Mrs. Cohen in geometry
Miami Beach Senior High in 1983

From orientation on, I don't know…
Mr. Moses was born on Christmas
He smoked a cigarette alone in his room
Why did they give us all that old English?
For me, advanced placement classes were a
    flourescent gloom
I don't want to say anything bad about Mr. Glick
There were things about him, though
That kind of made you sick
But everyone who took his classes knew their
    English lit

Forgive me
I was in the rock ensemble room
One of Mr. Burris's kids
I walked around in boots
Singing to myself a little bit

Okay, it was me; I confess
I spray-painted the school once or twice
It doesn't hurt to be nice
I didn't have enough to do, I guess
Rebel, rebel …
I'm still embarrassed
(But I'm O.K.)

I don't know…
I look back once in awhile
And I can feel the way I felt at the time
Like the sweet aroma my girlfriend wore that
   wintertime
I heard some rumors about me, even recently
That I'll neither confirm nor deny
But they say I'm into women's mud wrestling
What! How'd they know?

There's a lot to love about Miami Beach
A hundred blocks to ride and roam
And all your faces here tonight
Ain't it alright, our island home?
Happy New Year, motherfuckers!

I MISS HER, TOO

Mother, kiss your daughter
Mother got to weep
Father, oh father
See, he can't control his grief

Brother left the table
See, his face has turned to white
Sister looking at ya
Like you're a poisonous lookalike

Cages of our own making
And dreams the morning blinds
The dread at each day breaking
I know I 's once born in time
Yes, I know I was once born in time

July 2015

Having been "dismissed" from your practice
Dr. Wright, I'm sorry…
For something
I'm embarrassed and humiliated…
I guess

Why not a day spent together
At that museum featuring enhanced images
Of beasts from the African Serengeti plains?
(Gosh, in Jax!)

And why not a night out on the town
    around Jacksonville
At a crab shack with your six-year-old
Or conversation by candlelight
Somewhere in that ragtag metropolis?

I know I never went over the line
With any salaciousness or lascivious talk
Nope
No way!
That's not me
Cross my heart and hope to die
May I be eaten by a Yeti

Dr. Wright
You did an excellent job
On my rotten 48-year-old Bohemian mouth
Maybe I thought you needed a laugh…
Or simply just to get to know
Someone you've never known before
In that special way

I had a vision I should tell you about
Because we might not ever meet again

I was waiting at an intersection on my bicycle
And I leaned my head back and closed my eyes
I saw you in a black satin robe
You were rising out of jagged onyx
Small clouds of smoke at your knees
And at your ankles, tamed snarling flames
All that in a split second
I swear

Dr. Wright
I know all of this is strangely suggestive
But in what way I'm not sure

I'm gone from Jax now
And please be assured

That my loose infatuation would never affect my
  better judgment
I'm not going to show up and freak you out or
  anything…
At least, Dr. Wright, not until I'm driving
A dark colored very expensive Italian motorcar…
Then I might track you down

That, or, if I walk 400 miles up the state of Florida
I'll drop you a line when I'm a few days away
What do you do with a man who'd walk 400 miles
To kiss your sweet face…?

It was easy to see you and me
Running barefoot in blue jeans on the beach
In Hartley's laughter
I hope you find somebody to bring you such vibrance
  and joy
I really do

Tu sabes que yo tengo todo respeto para ti
La blanca petite españolita Doctor con ojos negros
  misteriosos

                                   —Maiche

BLIND SPOT SPELL

She got a fan shaped like Japan
He's got a farm
You can tell by his arms
I got a turkey with breasts so big
All she can do is rest
On a Kaiser roll with Muenster cheese
Yes, thousand island dressed

Stan's got a phone that won't leave him alone
Billy Joe's salamanders in their shades
They got all the answers
Mrs. Cow
To dance, she did not know how
One eagle said to the other
"You're my fall to the earth lover"
Nancy, the forest ranger
Was both friend and stranger

A lady carried a log
The DJ was God's own golden dog
The train was heavier than the station
The tracks proved their vocation
The rails were electric eels
Under platform heels
Paying the price of redemption

The psychic's table creaked
The pianist sat on the edge of her seat
The night watchman clicked his flashlight
Asked himself just who it was—
Him or them—who was really insane
Looked like something might not be right
The teacher's name was Rachel
The kids loved most dismissal
Carved their names in the table
The nurse never saw a woman more ready and able

The children ran according to size
The clouds showed a man with glasses on his eyes
Knee-high, they looked for mischief
Cutest thing you ever witnessed
And I heard the sweetest story you'll ever hear in
   this world
About an old man who once gave a locket to a girl
There was a flood in the south
Someone gave someone
A kiss on the mouth

The little transistor speaker shook to shake
A statue was unveiled
And the ground began to quake
Umbrellas and convertibles

Blow-dried hair
Big dates
The girl with pom-poms brought a book
She gave me a wink when I left in my boots
The chaplain spoke in a voice so plain
Peggy and Molly had unbelievably impacted cheeks
One rode a bike
One ate a burger at that place on the beach

Vern always showed
The lesson to learn
And said Bob
"Somewhere, all men are not slobs"

Albert
Someone helped him find the sweet spot
He said, "Hey!
I absolutely feel better
Lighter
Positively gay"

Linus and Freda…
So young at heart
Had a boy named Randy
The man at the store said, "I'll tell your mother
Stop stealing my candy"

Priscilla was Priscilla
Looked at me like I was Godzilla
Sean didn't come
He went to bed
He worked harder than anyone

Suzy wasn't a floozy
She said, "Here; have some more boozy
How 'bout you, Lucky?
Earl? Jake? Clay? Sparky?
Come on, Cousin Brucie"

Max gave his flask to Erica
They played in church under an exact replica
There was a big black fish at the aquarium
Who said he wouldn't work
'Cause they made him sleep in the bathroom
The cocker spaniel wouldn't bark
Put his paws over his ears
He left and went to bed with the old horse
Who loved biscuits with his beers

What's your name?
Where do you come from?
My name's Wilson Pickett

And I'm pretty sure I've just come
From the center of the sun

Let's read a poem by a man named Shel
He wears his hair on the inside of his skull
And he plays guitar pretty well

The principal was depressed
He knew he lacked purpose
You can't carry on a conversation at a tollbooth
In fact, the people in New Jersey think it
   highly uncouth

Shelley Schwartz loves sharks and urchins and eels
She loves sea lions and scallops and seals
And seaweed and conch fritters
My little mermaids and predators
A jellyfish stung her and a sea turtle bit her

I once knew a man from Nantucket
Moved to Arizona
Longed for Connecticut
Sharla sang songs at the local lounge
We walked our dogs at the park
She sure loved her scrounge

You should've heard 'IKE'
Howled at the open mic
Then there was Blaine
Blaine was his name
He worked a big yellow crane
He left the city; no opportunity remained

Matt finally found his voice
Gained 400 pounds
Moved to Detroit
Hey, isn't there a lot goin' down?
It's thrill to thrill here in Busytown
Waldo!
Wow! You're tall, man!

Faye
Your last name is Dunaway
She met a man who looked at her legs all day
Lauren Bacall
Your mother called
Chinaski?
Henry Chinaski…?

Hattie, you're a bit Chatty
I'll have to separate you from your friends
Mama was fifty-one years old

Gave birth to 9 childrens
You couldn't tell her anything
She didn't already know
Read lots of books
But never used words
With more than two or three syllables

Tom was a blonde, skinny guy
Walked clear to Micanopi
My ... a Spanish moon
Whoever wrote this must be crazy
Crazy as a loon
Spilt a glass of milk behind the TV
The broom was standin' tall in the kitchen
What'd ya put on a Kaiser Roll
With thousand island dressing?

At the corner store
A purplish man
Played a tabla drum
He was a tabla *drummer*
Fun
Then Tracy fell down
The track team gathered 'round
She was in good hands
So I went and sat down

I love hummus
I've eaten my weight of it
The white sauce is called "tahina"
I swear … I could drink it

If y' stay up all day and all night
Y' get smoke in your eyes
Y' get wired
Uptight
You could give someone a *bite…*
First date
I ate the green stuff on the plate
Japan took shape

Waiter…!
Is he gonna be alright?

DAH-DUMM

My favorite two are Goren and Eames
Like you, I've seen these detectives arrive at
And make their way through hundreds of
   crime scenes

What they can pull together
As the units plod on
Detection
A slight inflection
Top of the stairs
Bottom of the pond

They find a clue
When none are to be had
They're on the case
Undercover, they have a rare chemistry
All charm and good taste
Her dainty lass
The idiocies he achieves on that baby face

Yeah, detective Goren and detective Eames
He looks like he hasn't slept in a week
She's a pistol in her full-length leather coat

And all this
On those New York City streets

Sitting opposite a suspect in the interrogation
  room
Drama
Is it not highly memorable
The way they noodle a fella?

Detective Goren is given to reading the dictionary
When he's out on stake somewhere
In the back of a van
Detective Eames, Eskimo cute
She'll clear the deck right beside any federal man

Sometimes they're on a case
And Eames gets all riled
Goren right beside her
He has to cool her jets
Some all-important case-closing formerly irrel-
  evant trifle
Bobby and Erica questioning questions
Points of interest
Connecting the dots
A step ahead of the rest

Remember the episode that began on the
   Jersey shore?
Bales full of gold medallions had been found
Everybody had a little glitter on their fingers
A ship's ledger
A traitor's treasure
"Fish him out and take him down!"

It's practically a hobby
A convenient obsession
Law and Order: Criminal Intent
Nine hours it's been on in this hotel room
Mary Elizabeth Mastrantonio
Eric Bogosian
Ms. Yvonne
Rizzoli's cleft

Somewhere on a mound of earth overlooking New
   York…
The notables of *Law and Order* gonna be buried there
And all the great guest cameos
So well cast
They'll be ghosts in the cold night air

And there will be a big cement statue
Of Goren and Eames

At one of the gates
Captured in their trench coat Fogs
A DVD of all their seasons on a never-ending loop
A new episode … *God…*

"Okay, let me tell ya…
If I eva' encounta' Vincent D'Onofrio
Or whateva' his name is — Goren — on the streets
I'm gonna climb up his body
Till I'm huggin' his size-62 noggin, his *keppe*
Then I'll bite his ear
(Do you think that's queer?)
Bobby, you're not on duty
Let's go get a beer
He'd say, "Okay, man
I know this little jazz club on 5th
Right around the corner from here
Now man…
Can you please get of o' my shoulder!"

"And Eames
If I eva' meet up with that Erica
I will immediately go rob a bank
And bring 'er half a million dollas
Just so she'll have lunch wit' me an' th' boys back in
      tha' tank

Ohp!
That Dick Wolf has stolen
Yet anotha' perfectly good hour
Think I'll light up a cigar
Who's that sittin' in the corner at the counter?
Hey you ... You can't smoke in here!

And, hey, you know
I've always been onto Olivia and Stabler
Hey, it's not a brain drainer
It's a brain *enabler*
(Munch made a funny!)

Dr. Wong's marathon
Let's not forget Sam Waterston
Wait, Detective Jeffries is gonna be on
With that face someone stole
From the surface of the sun
Briscoe was a good man
"I got shoes older than you, son!
I got lucky once back in '87
Another club soda for everyone!
Don't ya love it here at Neilson's?"
9 o'clock Wednesdays
They clear out
And they're *gone*

BLOOD OF TIME

The blood of time
So thin it seeps
So thin it seeps
So thin it seeps
The blood of time
So thin it seeps
Upon the stones of my house of bricks
My house of bricks
My house of bricks

The mudd of time
So thick it sits
So thick it sits
So thick it sits
The mudd of time
So thick it sits
At both exits of my house of bricks
My house of bricks
My house of bricks

Tumblin' in time
You get your kicks
You get your kicks
You get your kicks

Tumblin' in time
You get your kicks
Ain't that a kick in the head?
Yes, it's a kick in the head
Yes, it's …

The blood of time
So thin it seeps
So thin it seeps
So thin it seeps
The blood of time
So thin it seeps
Upon the stones of my house of bricks
My house of bricks
My house of bricks

LIL SMARTASS

He once got beat up by a girl
She beat him about the head
On the wide raspberry sidewalk
In front of the schoolyard
On a Saturday

He'd called her sister "ugly"
And she'd cried all night
Could not be consoled
Missed school the next day

Big sister found the boy
And cut him off while he rode bikes
With his friend, David Stoneberg
And she walloped him *good*
She tightened her fist and swung sidearm
Busting his temples

A little old lady tried to stop the beating
But she went on slapping his ears
Which popped and started to ring

Sister stood off and came back at him
"Ugly!?"

The chain link fence hurt the back of his head
He was trembling
Too shook to whimper or cry out

The sun was white bright
He turned his head
And saw David across the street
In the drugstore entrance
With his palm above his head against the glass

We never looked her way twice again

CARING

Who cares?

What is caring?

I feel strongly about these things you're sharing

To care…

Might need two brains between your ears

Might need two lemon slices for both of your
    eye sockets

A lemon tree bears fruit for years and years

To care

Nextdoor neighbor says my music blares

How about scapegoats in the gardens of millionaires?

Grace

The cutting edge

Is lit up with flares

No peace at the apex

No peace in an infirmary full of soldiers

Care

The ghetto is proof of something

Let us share

The ghetto is half brotherly union

And half motherly tears

What goes on in there?

In all that blight
A moment's pleasure
Most of 'em ain't got two dollars
Bus to work and back from there

Caring
Does it come from behind a big oak desk?
Caring
Off the badge on Officer Friendly's chest?
To put yourself in someone else's shoes
You can usually tell when someone's paid their dues

Caring
You can shed a tear of care at the movies or
   on the radio
I can remember reading books when I was young
And the tears there were memorable
You'll shed a tear when one of your best
   friends goes
There was so much hope in him
I know angels will follow her wherever she goes

Dr. Benjamin Spock
And Dr. Ruth Westheimer
What you chose to suffer
What was okay to endure

To hear your laughter again in the bright sunlight
Y' know we only have so many calendars

Caring
You'll pause…
What you feel when your mother dies
This much she fared with a look of love in her eyes
After weeping
We go out doin' all the things we did before
Hopefully we collect the things we're better for

Caring
Well there's your degree in voyeurism
Where should we pin the star?
After you've been here with me
I don't want to know where you are
But wear your brown socks
And your private school bollocks
And count to ninety backwards

Caring
I'm playing "Hotel California" in a café in
    Tbilisi, Georgia
Everything's prefab gray
If I told you why I'm here, it'd be a lie I told ya
Anyway…

I love what she's wearing
It's cheap
And overbearing
Halters and garters and imitation fur
I ain't got one girlfriend
I got four!
And who cares?
No one

Caring

I Had a Friend, She

I had a friend, she
She was more like me than me
Did I leave her, or she me?
I had a friend, she

I went back
She was gone
No wait, she was there …
And everything went wrong
I sat on the curbside in the sun
What just happened?
A slip of the lip
A loose, angry tongue
What have I done?

Face in my hands
Melted Krügerrands
French Quarter crows
Royal Street woes
Undone in old New Orle-ans

Months on
I woke up on the other side of the earth

With a heart-shaped tattoo healin'
It covered a man up about 5 foot, seven
It don't take long to get tired
Of knocking on the doors of Heaven

I'd just had a dream of a man
Who kept lambs on the side of a rock-strewn
   mountain
He was bearded
He stepped out through blue tarps in the wind
I was bandaged
I was sore
Morning light beaming in

I found my way to a central bus station
I found my way to a psychiatric hospital
People my age were smearing pudding
On the screen of the TV that hung on the wall

The bulimic girl in black Converse was there
So was Uncle Jugular
There was a little turntable in the rec room
I listened to "Homeless"
And "Diamonds on the Soles of Her Shoes"
Someone handed me a telephone

And a friend from home asked me
If I'd heard of these Traveling Wilbury dudes

Here come my jetlagged folks
Both plagued and tired
Sometime later I sat at a conference table
Where a small league of doctors inquired
Well I must've said something like
"Gee, I had a friend
 She … really got to me."
Apple from lunch in my hand
"So, a lost love is why you did this to yourself,
    young man?"
 (munch)

 Yes, it was a desperate act
 Of desperate measure
"Tonight, you will dream of me," I prayed
 At 20 years of age
 I had to show the queen some treasure
 Worst move I ever fucking made

 On an outpatient basis
 I was released to a shabby little place
 In a shabby little neighborhood

People my age played Backgammon and board
   games
The fragrance of hashish in the air lightened
   the mood

The doctor was a rehab specialist from the Midwest
Somewhat the alcoholic I'd guess
In his cross-town spread
He saw his patients
I saw the title "Undefeated" in his library
Which was modest
Ceiling fan overhead
Halls with stone arches
Can't remember his name
Maybe it's for the best

One roommate was a war hero from Ireland
One had whooping cough
A young American
Another was a kind hearted, God fearing,
   South African
Another was ranting, raving, zealot material
Poised for the cover of Phillip Roth's next novel

The kitchen had dirt-flecked, flickering, fluores-
   cent lights

And beat up parquet floors
Welcome to Dr. So-and-So's
Little shop of horrors

Soon after arriving
I wrote a blues tune without a pencil or a pen
It was about my friend and our split
It was all a huge bluff
Sweet sentimental stuff
But it helped me out quite a bit
And I still have it
It's really rather exquisite.
And I'd let you hear it
But it puts me too over the edge
And I'm hardly in the mood anymore to even think
   of it
Let alone sing it
Maybe some day I'll remember to forget it

Oracle Magdalene chart topping hit
She picked out a burgundy crystal pyramid
Time's own bit
Entrances
Exits
Stages lit
Come sit

Chocolate?

Date?

Grape?

Pomegranate?

Davidka

David

For months afterward

All I could do was return to the memory of her im-
    perfect face

This deep voiced, bow-jawed woman

Had pretty much taken my place

Almond eyes

Thick braid high

Broken nose

Heaven-sent

All I could do was go deeper in a corner

Further into my closet

Which was where

And what

Led to these troubled events

A snow flurry fell

Late in the evening

I was in a T-shirt on the street

I caught a chill

I looked around at the apartments with lights
   comin' on
And I thought, *Nowhere do I belong here*
There's nowhere I belong
Some moments in your life
Are chill upon chill

I had a friend, she
Three years a senior to me
Told me her father was a farmer of flowers by trade
She had a copy of Stevie Nicks' "Bella Donna"
We drank tea she regularly made
She cracked her knuckles
And snored in bed
She looked at me
And quietly proclaimed a love for horses
In another town
In another time
I'd dreamt of constellations changing courses
Yes, constellations changing courses
We were special together …
Special …
Whatever

The empty-handed heart
So hard it all comes down

I didn't even look in the doorway
Last time I's in speakeasy town
Like a ship that's tied to an anchor
Anchor and chain must be hauled aboard
I still had jock itch from high school
I hadn't kissed a woman in three years or four
I'm not sure
Smoke gets in your eyes

The French Quarter's balconies
The latticework of gargoyles
That's enough tea
Now put the cream away
It's quick to spoil
She was all Silverman and Winehouse
Comfort enshrined
So much had been made so easy for me
To this day you can say
He's still very much resigned

She smiled once
When we first met
I turned around and right there
Such a widening set
She smiled twice
Walkin' with her on the way to work

Foolin' around on the sidewalk

Playin' the jerk

And she smiled on me

When she walked in

And I was singing a song off of "The Joshua Tree"

It was all too good to be true

Must 've been somethin' really wrong with me

I had a friend, she

She has known that all is vanity

The moment was tempting

She delivered me

To me

Like a prize of battle

Like a casualty of war

She left me standin' in the doorway

Cryin' in the parlor

"Pity have I," she said

For these weaknesses of yours"

She was a country girl

A foreigner

Here on those swampy American shores

Clawed mantle pieces and torn clothes

Empty coffee cups and too many cigarette butts

Strippin' away at it all

Preservation Hall
This seat is saved for a *Rumble Doll*

I know I'm not the only soul
Who's ever lost someone of their own ilk
Soul to soul
You'll give up your youth and your health
You'll even give up your rock 'n' roll

Roses are red
Violets are blue
Green apples
Corn kernels
Olive oil
Sugar cubes

I had a friend, she
As mythical as Hera to me
Must've crawled out 've a light-switch
Or come from the gulf of Mexicali
These sisters of mercy have come
The fool on the hill is more lonely than anyone
In broken times
Only the broken can you enlist
The only explanation I have for myself
Is that I do a lot of writing like this

I was barefoot
On a warm sidewalk in Miami
Some months on
'Come fallin'
These tiny brown leaves
Tiny brown leaves …
And I thought to myself
"Everybody calls y' baby down in New Orleans"

A woman
In an old fashioned bathtub singin'…
Doesn't know half the words
But keeps the tune
A slip of the lip
A parchment rip
Red skies at night
Changing dunes

That place had two big rooftop windows
One facing north
One facing east
I'm pretty sure at least
I bet a lot of people carried on
In that flat in the Quarter
Caught up to be bound
And never released

Sticks and stones will break your bones
But words do permanent damage
The St. Charles trolley
Runs from Old Canal Street
You can see the ghosts in the stacks
Clear down to Loyola College

I had a friend, she

Double Helix

Stillness

Cold

Darkness

Death

Stars shooting

Dust falling

Smoke rising

Speed

Veloce

Pace climbing

Heat cleansing

Form forming

Form breaking

Critical mass

Sun shining

Salt glazing

Rain falling

Seeds bedded

Roots taking

Genesis

Blood flowing

Blood coursing

Touch…

Feeling…

Mouths speaking

Steps coming

Horns butting

Hooves clopping

Slings hurling

Cups holding

Wheels spinning

Fires ablaze

Dreams…

SHHHH

Sounds like the ocean crashing
The papers rustlin'
The pencils tap and seethe the same
Sand paper
Grit
Static

Shhh…
The sound of whispering children
A last deep breath before jumping in
A beanbag dragged across the floor
The cigarette is silent; the lighter isn't
A snake in the grass
A showerhead's blast
Five o'clock New York City slush
Me, you dare shush?

Shhh…
Put this shell to your ear
You can hear…

TO CATCH A SHARK

To catch a shark
By light or dark
Coral reef underneath
Wild beast
Skin
Teeth
Salt
Senses
I can catch you a shark in five minutes
I can catch a shark for what fifty cents is

To catch a shark
Night is black
Day is blue
Monster
Nature
Structure
Polar
Lunar
Solar
Latitude and longitude
Sir, this shark steak's for you?

To catch a shark
Bait: chum
Mate: one
Knife: blood
Billy club
Wet deck
Gaff net
Flappin' fin
Slappin' in
Captain!

An expensive bowl of soup
A picture on a desk
Long lined
Plunge-spined
Maligned
'Jaws' sign
Prehistoric
Philharmonic
Kill it!
It's just a shark
What the heck?

Chair mount
Quint's count

Quint's song
"Dead Calm"
Jeans on
Rough palm
Fish On!

To catch a shark
Tackle box
Rods 'n' reels
Butter crackers
Ice 'n' beers
Coca-Cola
Orange peels
How the rolling boat feels

Line hit!
Surface
Wahoo?
Kingfish?
Set it!
Snag it!
Reel it!
Blacktip got it!
Dammit!

Dollar bets

You're one on the throat

You're two on the neck

To catch a shark

Hooks, leads

Wires, pliers

High noon

Harpoon

Time set

Filament

Red gill

Cool spray

Big, eh?

Taxidermy

Way t' go, l'il Johnny!

To catch a shark

Boat's beam

Stern's gate

Crests

Falls

Pull

Wait

Ugly stick

Captain Rick!

Ok now people, stand away from the tip!

Journey done

Mile million 'n' one

'Neath the moon

'Neath the sun

Dead and gone

Sharkdom

To catch a shark

Heave tide

Ease ride

Rowed teeth inside

Leopard spots

Tiger stripes

Swims right up and takes a bite

To catch a shark

Pylons, piers

Seasons, years

Bays, bridges

Depths, ridges

Currents, tides

Not up 'n' down

They swim side to side

Mystic Bill

Sharks kill

Feed

Strike
A shark!
Yikes!

CRACKHEADS

First thing a crackhead does when he comes inside
    your house
Is to look for something he can put in his pocket
A pack of cigarettes, a pen, anything … a watch, your
    wallet
Later on you look; you can't find it; you think you've
    lost it

Second thing a crackhead does when he comes inside
    your house
Is to crave what he needs, what he's begged
You make a pot of coffee, you pour a glass of juice
"You got any whiskey and shit, instead?"

Third thing a crackhead does once you let him in
    your house
He becomes morose and dour
He's unsettled and fidgety, can't sit still
"Man, you got a few dollars?"

Fourth thing a crackhead does having crossed the
    threshold of your home
He'll start groveling, lowdown judgment on you

About how little you know, and the soft way of life
you chose
Blows his nose in your Terry Cloth blue

The fifth thing a crackhead does when you've taken
him out of the rain
He'll sleep till the following afternoon.
You've got things to do
But there's someone on the other side of your
living room

The sixth thing a crackhead does once ensconced
inside your house
Is to lie back and use the phone
He'll say "Hey man I'll get to the dishes in the sink"
You and your dog are no longer alone

The seventh thing a crackhead does
Is to shake your generous hand and smile
A little insanity in his eyes
Maiche, it's been there all the while

And the last thing a crackhead does from the com-
fort of your home
Is pack his bags and get *gone*
He's got $900 worth of your prized CDs
He'll get $55 for them down at the pawn

MARGO

Margo,

If you knew what my mind twists up for you
You would take me out of your pocket
And come play with me again

This mean sun…
Do you still have it in you to wrap me up like you
   once did?
Those straw platforms splashing in the street
A writer always needs someone to read to
I'm here for a while…

                            —ML

P.S. Do you still have Rusty's number?

RIGHTEOUS DAYDREAM

How we gaze when we ponder
How we look away when we think
How a voice can be so soft
And then turn metallic

How laughter is sweet
How laughter is lit
When forced, laughter cackles
Cackled laughter
The Bible talks about it

It's a beautiful world but hatred seethes
If you can take a breath you've got a right to breathe
Come, come now
What with all this talk about a "right to exist"
To engage your enemy in a full-blown drawn out
    scrimmage

The sun and the moon and the wind
And the rain and the incidental saint
Y' been shown new direction
And given new dreams
All about the way it is
And the way it ain't

Here I am
Sun's come up
Clean and sober
Pretty much
Your day will be about the regards you hold
    for others
And things like juggling, surfing, and two-hand
    touch

Evil knows not itself
Evil must handle
There might be more to stand up for
Than in any table of choices
There's no one around
And every once in a while I get a head full o'
    foreign voices

How we gaze when we ponder
How we look when we think
Isn't it miraculous, basic memory?
The involuntary
To flinch
To blink

How we gaze when we ponder
How we look away when we think

Yeah, we're bound to spend some time
Rumbling around the rink

How we gaze when we ponder
How we look when we think
If you're so smart, Joan of Ark
Won't ya give them heels a clink

I WISH

I wish there was a gardenia plant around here
I wish there was a fresh water lake in this town
I wish I knew how to clean a fish
Serve a busy lady a tasty dish
Coffee and cream on a side street in town
Spanish guitars
Our cantina's deep dark sounds

Wish my mother to live a hundred years
Wish my long lost lover knew the time and tears
Wish I'd never left my wife
She's the best thing that ever happened to me in
    this life
Wish this world wasn't bent on revenge
But it is, this world is revenge hinged
Wish I lived at the end of a friendly cul de sac
There'd be no disgruntled old girlfriends
Holdin' cheap platform shoes by the straps
Jenny, palmin' a baseball bat

I wish my laundry was folded
The dishes done
Floors mopped
Rugs dusted

Windows clear

Kitchen sink

Tub scrubbed

Top to bottom

Bottom up

Wish I was on some Australian mountain range

I got no reason to be there

But I imagine it would be some kind of change

Wish I didn't have to finally give her up

'Bout the time we would've flown free

Right about the time the poor girl began to recon-
  sider me

We practiced a form of emotional abuse

A chess game of ever deepening cruelty

Wish I wasn't given to talking to myself
  so virulently

So menacingly

So threateningly

Pathetically

Existentially

Hello…

It's me

I wish I knew who Ayn Rand was

Or maybe I don't

She writes all about New Orleans, right?

Hokey as hokey as hoke

Emergency rooms are filled with 15-year-old girls

With neck bite wounds

Ayn, there lies the mighty Mississippi

On her shores, sinking shacks

They hunt in packs

An' this a N' Orleans tune

Hit it!

I wish you knew how little it means to me that you
    don't make contact

I wish you knew how scrambled I get each time you
    come back

A memorial

An anniversary

The world's most catastrophic shopping spree

I wish you could feel some of what I've felt

Been forever since I filled a page with wishes

But why not?

It fills you with a spirit of childishness

Wish I didn't know now what I didn't know then

Wherever you're coming from

Whatever century you're livin' in

There's a lot of things we didn't do
That I wish we had
But then…
Where would she have to go to after she's been
   so bad?

And don't ya just *hate* it
When you confide in someone
And the very next day…
What's being said
Is just that smart and insightful and enthralling
Sometimes you don't know if you're dealing with
   the dead

I wish I was eight years old
And the big kid on the block was like Tom Petty
Talkin' and lookin' on that way
We'd fish in the canal
Bait our hooks with strips of hamhocks
Lick our fingers
All greasy with hickory
He'd have a picture of a naked lady in his pocket
   that'd make my eyes bug out
We'd catch a mess of little bream and leave 'em
Ride our bikes to the store
Steal some gum and go runnin' out!

So let's put this board game back in the box

And put the box back in the closet

And put these kids to bed

I'll take the ties out of your hair

On the dresser, a gardenia flower

Lamp down low

Window's night air

And I'd touch your face with my fingers

And we'd meet eye to eye

And we'd rejoice having a lifetime to spend together

You and I

I wish

NEVER WRITE POETRY

I'm standing in the hall
I'm lying on my bed
I'm in the bath
I'm in the middle of the room
Hands clasped behind my head
There's nothing in the fridge
My forehead to the wall
I'm starting to pace
I'm holding the cat
I'm smoking

I'm standing in the hall
Thinking of not nine
But ten-thousand yesterdays
Counting myself among the casualties
The depths of turbulence
Never serve burgundy at a séance
Never covet one who's covetous of elegance
Especially if she's boyish
Doggish
Piggish
Bearish
Shortish

She may or may not be Jewish
I'll get in trouble for this

Hey! Who ordered Uncle Milty's whitefish?

BITTER HEART

I've got a bitter, bitter heart
Till the end of the day from the start
Bitter behind the eyes' stinging pool
Mirror shows I am my own somebody's fool

A bitter, bitter heart
Like a schoolboy whose girl has taken it away
One thing he knows
Life ain't at all the same
What flew before, it don't fly today
Could we have treated each other right, anyway?

A bitter heart
What are the facts?
They poke and chide
Chide and poke
What we'd like to reveal the least
What we'd like not to share the most
It strikes me as more than a reminder
I turn away
With only one wish…
To find her
Woe is me

Who's the devil
He or she?

Bitter
Came in feeling one way
Left feeling another
Can't stand the company of men
Mr. Bojangles loved his dog more than his brother
All this sorrow is too much pain
All this guilt I've been wallowing in
This existential shame
What was he supposed to do?
She was lost on the merry-go-round
To transgress
To regress
To digress
To trespass
If every time it was…
I hit the ground

Bitter as one who hates his life and what he's done
    to it
How did you become a patient?
I never figured out if I was too good for you
Or you were too good for me
I got a ticket to a third-world country

And a suitcase full of sesame candies
In my time of dyin'
Lord will take me
From this life no man's apt to live
Close out this point of view
Cancel this perspective
Love's not an evil thing
No harm done
Nietzche said, "A joke is an epigram on the death of
   a feeling"

Bitter
Comes a time when you're tested
When you can't do what you do best
When you find you've been bested
Bitterness
Like the kid in his dorm room who was with
   another man
He walked straight to the Brooklyn Bridge
And threw himself in
There's no embrace
No step to dance
Can't imagine a kiss
I'll probably make two-hundred-million dollars
And then be called upon to live with all this
The man who gains the world but loses his soul

What sin's worth these wages?

Bitter

From a well with water so rank nobody can drink

Oh, Oh Michaela

Do I need your permission to turn the other cheek?

We're sometimes the angel

Sometimes the demon

A man's word

Some women prove all the malcontent of
    femininity

Milestones

Seems all I'm comfortable with is going home alone

All the places I've been

All the places you left

He joined the French Foreign Legion to gain
    her respect

Bitter is sad and mean

Everybody gets bitter from time to time

Everybody can prove themselves the criminal kind

What's there in that life of yours

That ever called out to this life of mine?

I can't stand company

Can't stand to be alone

The things we put each other through

How could you…?
How could *I?*
How could *you?*

Bitter
Bitter enough to ask, "Should we part?"
Bitter
Sick at heart
She got on a plane
He sat in the dark
Issues…
Come what may
Bitter
So bitter no tongue can tell
No words can say
Bitter as taking to the road alone
Bitterness—the grindstone
What it is to have to pick up the pieces and go home

HIGH SCHOOL IN ISRAEL MEMORY

We sat in hollow metal-framed wooden chairs
We were sixteen and seventeen
The subject was "dehumanization"
3:30 a.m. to breakfast
Yogurt, coffee, breads, greens

American kids on hormones of their own
We were there to learn how to *learn*
Student to teacher ratio is everything, Jones
Sunny classroom
Sunny desert
In a white and red bus
I remember…
Sandy, hot, dry, thirsty afternoons

Next day to the fields
Vines of grapes
Snips at dawn
The first birds at sunrise singing their sunrise song
Shower
Change
Sandwich
Language
Curriculum

Each student was assigned and received welcome
In the houses of families throughout
The town of Hod Hasharon

My roommate squeezed a cutie
I was sleeping alone
Matt Pincus came in and said
"Let's go drink some vodka"
Neil Young in his headphones

My adopted home housed an older middle-aged
   woman
Who'd lost her daughter some years before
In the north
To a knife
A lone assassin set upon her
From behind a boulder
Put an end to her precious life

A grieving mother in time
This appointment I'd have to keep
She kept a rag in her hand
Dabbing her eyes
I'd be there
She was alone
Softly she'd weep

The night

Onyx

The day as bright as thin

There's never a cloud in Tel Aviv

You're just below the sky in Jerusalem

This isn't a travel brochure

When you're there, you're largely on your own

What the disenfranchised and powerless will try

You're not in Cairo when you're teeing up in Dubai

To whom is this land home?

Largely on your own…

I was a few years younger

Than her daughter had been

At the time of her murder

I went to the house a few times

And sat with her

Glad to sweep up and mop her floors

This wounded woman's eyes never stopped tearing

She helped me learn the alphabet of

Ancient Hebrew lettering

Into what realms does a grieving mother ask "why?"

The will to begin

To get out of bed

To even try

There is nothing so cruel as to bury a child
You'd give anything for it to be you, instead

The killer may have been pressured
Extorted from within
Was he paid four-hundred dollars?
A small fortune
Dehumanization
Or maybe he acted alone?
A brother's avenger
The cycle of violence
A female
A teenager
A soldier

Summer came
And I could have lingered there
But I went home for my senior year
I got a job in a bakery that summer
I was smokin' menthols
Back in my world
And it was a long while
And lots of laughs later
That I thought of her there
We sat in class

All of sixteen or seventeen

Finding out what the word "dehumanization" means

The rabbi's apartment was no grand affair

Of bright and shiny things

Books wall to wall

And baby toys everywhere

We came to revere him

He was serious

But he could *laugh*

I'd like to go visit him

See what became of it all

High School in Israel

THE GIRL UP IN TOM'S RIVER

There's a girl up in Tom's River
Your breath, her voice could steal
There's a girl up in Tom's River
Of stately fine appeal

There's a girl up in Tom's River
She sings in sweet vignettes
There's a girl up in Tom's River
A dancer, a pianist

There's a girl up in Tom's River
Played shadow to his ghost
That girl up in Tom's River
Met her at a Greyhound outpost

There's a girl up in Tom's River
I'm not gonna tell you her name
There's a girl up in Tom's River
I can't tell you, I love the dame

That girl up in Tom's River
Poor friends, poor family
That girl up in Tom's River
She's in the penitentiary

The girl up in Tom's River
You'd break her to hold her too strong
The girl up in Tom's River
What could she have ever done wrong?

That girl up in Tom's River
I remember her, oh so well
That girl up in Tom's River
My my, that girl sure was swell

Gonna go see that girl in Tom's River
And kiss her face 23 times
Gonna go see that girl in Tom's River,
Look into her eyes while she looks into mine

Oh Chelsea, Oh Chelsea Bergen
I'd rob a bank and bring you the coin
Oh Chelsea, Oh Chelsea Bergen
How long 'till we be readjoined?

Chelsea, Oh Chelsea Bergen
Sweet like a jumping bird
Chelsea, Oh Chelsea Bergen,
Oh, the things my wife hasn't heard

There's a girl up in Tom's River,
She knows the town where I roam
The girl up in Tom's River
At the diner right near my home

HEADSHEET

Maiche Lev

Male
And never kissed or wished to be kissed by one
(No offense to anyone)

Born in a blizzard at night
In the front seat of a Chrysler
The same model used in the Steve McQueen movie
   Bullitt
(I'm that cool)

February 3, 1967
Beantown
Not the summer of love, but the winter of disgruntle-
   ment
Someone was strangling women in the neighbor-
   hoods

I was in the Cub Scouts for an hour
After a full day of listening and "behaving"
More of the same just wasn't gonna happen
(No way)

I stuck my finger in the cat's ear
When I was four or five
I'm not sure

I used to make sure the door was locked
When I humped the shaggy shower rug

The Vietnam War was a bloody event on TV
I saw enough of it at age five or six
To cause me to be afraid of both war and death
And I distinctly remember that thing called
   "the draft"
Everyone goes
That bothered me
At five or six

I grew up in the burbs of Miami Beach
With an affectionate-enough, hard working,
   internist for a father
And a worrying, beauty of a lamb, med-tech for
   a mother
She read novels endlessly
And he loved tennis and the ponies
Both my folks are non-drinkers
There was no physical abuse in the house
Both were Virginia-born-and-raised
And spoke with that state's soft southern accent

We built things, my dad and I
Where other fathers didn't
We built boats for the canals
Serious competition go-karts
(I used to mess with the speed screw; threw every-
    thing off)
Acetylene torches, Skil-saws, sanders

My mother sent me nearly twenty care packages at
    sleepaway camp one summer
She fed us early breakfast Monday thru Friday
She fed us dinner the same
And she put in an eight-hour day in Dad's Miami
    Beach offices
I shudder to think how much I'll miss her
Sometimes they still laugh heartily watching TV
    together
They're in their 80s

Two sisters
Both a little older
Both Scorpios
Both with record collections I benefitted from
Crosby, Stills, Nash, and Young's "So Far"
I remember trying to sing "Helplessly Hoping" and
    "Cost of Freedom"

And "Suite Judy Blue Eyes" was *everything*
And steely Dan's "Can't Buy a Thrill"
On 8-track and Vinyl
Most valuable lesson ever learned?
Really?
It's not hard to devalue and cheapen
The richness your birthright entails

Second most important lesson ever learned?
Seasickness comes on fast
And lasts a long time

What gets your goat?
It's an unfunny thing
For the dull to label the gregarious, "manic"

I attended public schools and religious school
    in Miami Beach
If I didn't have a radio by my desk
And a girlfriend on the phone
I probably would have been more than a
    mediocre student.
(Hail, Hail, Rock 'n' roll)

Any prejudices you'd mention?
I'm free of prejudging things; I am
And I know I am

I don't need to prop my race up
By calling another's "poor" or "lesser"
Liberty is just equality in school
Everybody knows that

Ever meet anybody famous?
I have a first cousin who races Intel Cup NASCAR
   series…
And you don't!
Reid Sorenson, a Georgia boy
Ran top-five at Daytona twice

My earliest memories?
   A) Hot sand! Hot sand!
   B) My aunt Leona's cookies and the waxed paper
      inside the tin they came in
   C) Fishing off Virginia Beach Pier with Grandpa
      Lewis at night
   D) I have an uncle who gargles with Tobasco sauce

Pet peeves?
I hate parades
Running out of Half-and-Half
Gnat swarms while biking
The meticulousness required by all things
   computer-driven
(I'm worse than your mother)

Last book I read?
Something about Amazonian Indians
Whose women enjoy fertility into their seventies
By eating mushrooms
(Yes there was an Anaconda scene)

My idea of God?
The essence of God is all around us
Everywhere, mountain and molehill
One must live in part to be able to accept oneself
   in death
You *can* move on
And eventually forgive yourself anything
If you can give yourself a good talking to
God is in the lychee nut
The mango
The pinecone
His orgasm must be the monarch butterfly's
   migration

What impact do you think your writing might have on
   the general reading public?

Well, I'd say that writing is—in and of itself—
A very potent neurochemical balancer

For both reader and author
Eventually, however briefly
We know and see the things we refuse to know
   or see
Where was I at?
What was I made of as the travails of life started to
   plague my soul?
What was I reading at the time?
What was in my ears?
It hasn't been a completely unpleasant trip at all
Deep emotional turmoil aside
Bono said:

  "Every artist is a cannibal
  Every poet is a thief
  All kill their inspiration
  And sing about their grief"

I got high for twelve years after my divorce—
And on cheap shit, too
Only three times in thirty years
Have I tried to write while high
It doesn't work for me
I always find myself "over the top"
It's a wonder I'm not "spun" or dead

I haven't answered the question: Impact…? Public?

So much is so poorly written in the field of
   songwriting
(Michael Stipe said that)
Where poetry is shared
Heard
There are no TVs on
For a finite time
Before it becomes too grating
People read something they've written
That's a good thing

I find Metallica's demagoguery
To be as empty as the Junior High School garages it
   stems from…
Sorry, guys
Please don't kill me
I've still got a lot left to do

Please…
The rhythm and blues slickness
Is as godless as it is self-congratulatory
This brand of vain suffering
Is the truly masturbatory
(Smokey's still the man, though

"One Heartbeat" is a sweet number
And who can resist Marvin's "Sexual Healing?"
And Rita Coolidge is God)

 Outside, the rain begins
 And it may never end…

Writing…
The closest I come to "Gonzo"
Is saying "fuck" every once in a while — or "shit"
I should read more
Everybody should have an editor
Poetry is a hard sell
I was gonna go on a long bike ride today
But I'm sitting here writing
Might as well

What's the first thing you ever took pride in writing?
I was in the fourth or fifth grade
It was a book report on the life of
 Thomas Alva Edison
I put it in a folder and everything
I remember being proud of my determined
 handwriting
It was in pencil
The cover was dark blue

Anything you'd like to hide?
Uh … what kind of fucking question is that?

I had a dark night about thirty years ago
I've written about it
I hope those few kids out there will be smarter
How much do you think a jealous monk's
    literary work
Might be worth?
Maybe it is that all I ever do
Is walk around reciting some strange alphabet
Where do you love to go?
To be in the surf in a heavy, heavy rain
Life is good

Sheryl Crow is the urethra of rock 'n' roll
(Her whole band is from Chicago)

A guy who looks a lot like a younger version of me
Opened up the Live-Aid concert in Philadelphia
On July 13th, 1985
But it's really the comedian Paul Riser's nephew,
    Bernard

Jerry Garcia has no equal
And never will

Jacob Dylan has great, soulful pop music sensibilities
"Red Letter Days" gets me goin'
"Somebody Else's Money" off of his first album is also
   a personal favorite
The intro feels like Mozart's piano had a mouse in it

While on the subject of favorites…
The Counting Crows song, "Long December"
Is one of the greatest songs you could ever ask for
It was probably written in five minutes
Funny…
My first wife and I went to a Black Crows concert
I think they were warming up for the Heartbreakers
After the show she looked at me with a face
That women get after a deeply orgasmic experience
Chris Robinson and his brother must have that effect
   on unsuspecting people with girl-parts, everywhere
She said she'd go see them anytime

I saw Prince in the mid 80s
He walked on-stage on an Easter Sunday
With a full moon rising over the Miami Orange Bowl
And he said
"I'm here to play with you"
A girl in front of us was very upset about having lost
   her brush

Matthew Sweet's "Smog Moon…"

Learn it! Know it! Love it!

Predictions for the future?

The agnostic spirit will not stand

And I believe that North America will become

A scattered series of islands

An archipelago if you will

Sorry…

You asked…

Land ho!

My name is Maiche Lev

VICTORIA'S

The dark avocado

The lit lantern

The full tangerine

The orchid

The hibiscus

Bold

Beautiful

Feminine

A luscious woman

Her sultriness

She's a night in a forest

A morning garden

To be close enough to touch her lips

To put your own to them

Victoria in front of an ocean

Victoria in the mountains

Dawn beyond the horizon

See, the world *is* round

I haven't sat this way in so long with anyone

Once in a while I can tell what people were like

When they were children

It's a magic moment
It just happens

Victoria is the one who makes the magic carpet fly
Girls like that always got a guy
Forty-something
Mediterranean
That northern stem
A gypsy queen
The Black Sea's gem

Victoria
The hibiscus
The avocado
The pumpkin
The tangerine
Bold
Beautiful
Feminine
One of them

You're Her...

You're her bumpy puppy
You're her bell ringer
Her rocket over Snake Canyon
Her shaken, not stirred
Her ace in the hole
Her *yawp*
Her growl
Her roar
Her Mr. Fix-it
Her just-do-it
Her sweet and sour
Her hotcakes by the hour
Her personal trainer
Her Gloria Gaynor
Her don't-be-a-complainer

Her tamale toaster
Her rump roaster
Her juicy juicer
Her director and producer
Her fire
Her little white liar
Her Dapper Dan
Her sharp-dressed man

Her party thrower

Her lawn mower

Her good slap in the face

Her kiss in a public place

Her I never knew a love like this before

Her hard desire

Her foolish pleasure

Her I'd rather…

Her children's father

Her hunter-gatherer

Her boop-boop-bee-doo

Her do that to me one more time

Her this man on my arm; ain't he fine?

Her Sweet Daddy Mac

Her walking heart attack

Her rocket to the moon

Her one who calls the tunes

Her walk in the park

Her laughter in the rain

Her flint

Her spark

Her fireworks technician

Her doctor's orders

Her wish she still goes wishin' for

Her full-length leather jacket

Her Cape of Good Hope

Her baby, let me have it

Her hour of power

Her feeling dope

Her little devil

Her sweet bourbon daddy

Her sock-it-to-me

Her Jiffy Lube

Her righteous dude

Her fool wrapped around her finger

Her take anything you want from me

Anything...

Her express lane

Her caught in the act again

Her rooftop Duvalier

Her brushed swede

Her be a good boy

Her someone to annoy

Her fingerpainter

Her cherry picker

Her us against the world

Her coffee creamer

Her steamy steamer

Her dreamy dreamer
Her latest trick

FOLDED

If there was a way to fold time
I'd be up on it soon
Like in that film, *Dune*
Only no monster behind the glass
Minus the tubes
Cocoon

If there was a way to fold time
Like in that scientist's silver car
If there was a way to fold time
In the bathroom of this midtown bar
I'd stand in line
With all these useless friends of mine

The Curious Case of Benjamin Button
Born to be ninety years old
Mama still thought I was somethin'
I'd play piano
Forget football
Would take a while
Before I treasured a real live wholly livin'
N'awlin's *River Queen* doll

Hmmmmm…
To fold time…
I'd build a tollbooth
Put it about … *here*
Charge the folks a dollar-and-a-half to pass by
Ante up, drivers!

If there was a way to fold time
I'd 've made sure to be George Washington's next-
    door neighbor
I'd 've made myself into Salvador Dali's heartlessly
    impulsive lover
I could step right in and be the first person to put a
    loaf in a bread slicer
Me!

I'd grow a beard for show and tell
I'd show the cocky of this world the gates of hell
I'd discover the Talking Heads
And play drums for Blue Oyster Cult
At the Olympics I'd win the decathlon
My event — the catapult

If there was a way to fold time
All the emotional pain of this world

Would be easy to skip
And I wouldn't have my way just to have my way
I'd show up right on time
Every time
There'd be none of this life
Of bein' given the slip

La-dee-da
Another day
Children acting as children will
Y' know this town is the home of the Blue Angels
Jets fly fast enough to make the second hand stop
And the big hand turn to a quarter-till
The countertops shake and the Bloody Marys spill
All the people on the pediatric floor
Get up and walk to the windowsill
To fold time…

TREES

This tree
If y' eat from it
How smart you'll be
That tree
You'll be able to fly
If you grind its leaf 'til powdery

Potatoes don't grow on trees
Potatoes come from a potato plant
Rubber bands don't grow on trees
But they come from a rubber tree plant
You can try to move one but y' can't
Nope

Some trees bear fruit
That turns from green to yellow to red
Must be we'd 've never seen 'em ripe instead

I've heard of a tree that grows money
But I've never seen any
That tree there has stood eight hundred years
Trunk's as wide as a bus
So tall you can see it from here

There was a tree outside my window
Like an old friend to greet
"Hello there
I'm finally home
My, how you've grown"
Or "Farewell, friend
How your leaves have blown"
That tree made my whole street

A tree's summer fling
Begins in late spring
A tree loves fall
Finally needs a shawl
Winter would seem black and cruel
But winter's the time trees sleep
Quiet, still, and cool

That tree was called 'the giving tree'
You wouldn't believe what it gave
Now it's just a stump
A place to rest my rump
How noble a way for a tree to behave

That tree's got rings
That tree's got burrs
That tree bursts with sweet flowers

That tree has carobs that fall in the yard
Mean old man come and cut it down
'Cuz he felt he had to work too hard
(*Delonix regia*)

Trees grow
How it happens, nobody knows
Prickers and briars and thorns and spikes
Once…
On TV…
I saw a weed from Venus that actually *bites*

I could go on and on talkin' 'bout trees
But this pencil made of wood
Says anyone could
So …
Maybe everyone *should*
Write a poem
For something so perfect as a tree

A WREATHE

I don't know you from Adam, man, but I'm sorry
I'd been writing like never before
In a genre that could be no less the unfamiliar
I'm sorry
It happens
This song goes out to those I've offended
Loose ended
Sideswiped
I'm sorry
It happens

I called my teacher a name but I don't remember a
    thing
Maybe she wasn't so bad
Maybe she suffered from a vitamin deficiency?
She made a habit of being less than nice to me
But I don't remember a thing
Maybe she wasn't so bad

The boys at NASA need something to do
Need something to do
Yes, the boys at NASA need something to *do*
Brooks Brothers and topsiders

Shopping
Our mamas' very favorite thing to do

I never was a bully
I never was a victim, either
The 24-hour rule says
"Put it down for a day
Take a breather"
So put it down for a day
And take a breather

A bitter tree sheds bitter seeds
Can't this all be put to rest?
'Cause these bitter trees
Grown from these bitter seeds
Strangle the forest

I don't know you from Adam, man, but I'm sorry
I'd been writing like never before
In a genre that could be no less the unfamiliar
I'm sorry
It happens
This song goes out to those I've offended
Sideswiped
Loose ended

I'm sorry

It happens

AMERICA WITHIN SOME

To live in a town with three miniature golf courses
Pizza shops and those tee shirts of late
There are parallel zipcodes
All over the state
Mushrooms, onions, peppers, and anchovies on a
    white paper plate

The teams stand proudly assembled
The national anthem is being sung by a half-drunk
    woman at a piano
Her dress a little too low slung
Halftime show: the likes of Ted Nugent
Annie, get your guns

It's race day, boys
And you've got to know we won't catch spit off of this
    car
The fuel we've ended up with come from somewhere
    in Delaware
So swap some paint, superstar
Let 'em know you're there
Goddammit
Let 'em know who y' are!

I've heard it's twenty-seven pounds of sugar
Consumed individually per year
That any average citizen's sold
Crunchy, tasty, sticky, chewy
Dusty shelves of wrapped-up Tootsie Rolls
"Are you tryin' to score points with me?
You brought me Krön!"
Give the girl a kiss with a mouthful of Toblerone

Papa got a sweet tooth
Mama's jellyroll
Nutty Buddy comin' 'round the corner
"You won't eat your dinner
And she cooked her tuna casserole"

Surely all down the line
"Privilege" is the 'P'-word
Privilege
Word
I guess they front!
Outta luck
Wild pitch
Runner's going!
Rose is taking third!

There is no philosophy to be found
In sleeping behind a dumpster in a parking lot
Lord, don't let me become one of those
Who just could not get it right
Left to rot
Look sharp
Suck in that gut!

The new season
Woman can't stand the man
Man is full of complaint
It's all an ongoing assault
An unopened invitation to some further restraint
Good God, Magnum
What would reasonable foreigners think?

You can talk about change
Till you're blue in the face
Stay outta people's way here
And don't do too much talkin'
(California to the New York Island)
We are what we've allowed ourselves to become
America within some

MORNING SUN, MOURNING SON

A life worth living…
Confession, disclosure
Here y' blew your top
Here you lost composure

Had her callouses scraped
Up on Rodeo Drive
God, I love California,
Makes me feel so alive

There was somebody killed
By the Town Hall light
Ten years ago on a cold dark night
All the folks that were there
They all did agree
The man they saw runnin'
Looked a lot like me

You went fishin'
Caught a big one
These waves
These merciless waves
This sun
This relentless sun
I'm not gonna go next time I come

I Am Rumpelstiltskin

I am Rumpelstiltskin
And I've just stepped on a thorn
I was walking down to the river
Where I'm in till it's almost warm

They're not your friends
The secretive ones
Always asking for things
When they're gone
If it didn't come down to me like it did
I wouldn't own this nice, pretty farm, kid

I am Rumplestiltskin
And I've just stepped on a thorn
I was walking down to the river
Where I'm in till it's almost warm

Dreams and Visions, Voices and Moments With an Elusive Partner

Surfside

Sidewalk

Loggerhead

"These rock 'n' rollers"

Your little smile

With freckles

So close

The jumpy girl in the dining car

On the moving train

Behind glasses

Upstate

The girl in suede, low-cut boots

Half an aisle over

Out of Deerfield

My sleepy head bobbing

In one of my sister Jan's childhood friends'

Modest but modern and roomy homes

In a dream

I was led to a man

Who was standing though asleep
He woke up and screamed in my face

Same train
Different day and direction
Reading glasses on
"Too cute"
I'm sorry

By the bedpost in Boynton Beach
A voice whispered
"Because you're evil"
My response:
"You couldn't be talking to me"

The word "duplicate" or "replicate"
Something about trading places
Inaudible words spoken by another in my head

Being called a racist
Well, woman is the nigger of the world
John Lennon said that, if you don't know
He and George Wallace
Louis Farrakhan
And Al Sharpton
Could all share a cup of tea

On Mahatma Gandhi's grave
He wasn't buried in England
He was buried in India
And your boyfriend
Has as much going for him
As the third bottle of Bacardi
You gladly keep pouring
Then we could be friends
Ride 'em, cowgirl

"Listen…"
I sat still listening
What is all this telepathy an achievement of?
Or proof of?
Yes, sometimes I hear you
But it's always an invitation
To self-annihilation
Or is that just me?
This sickness
Referencing and re-referencing these long-since-
    dreamt skits
Someone got ahold of my heart
You've got a tight connection to my heart
Have a heart
My life is somewhat the ruined event
And I know it

I'm sorry to myself
I'm sorry for myself
To know what it means
Not accepting the failure
And hating you for making me hate you
I'm an astonished four-year-old
And I always have been
One is the loneliest number

The subway on 125th Street
Sixteen years…
Twelve of which I stood in line
Holding my own hand
Six-inch whole-wheat smothered-in-onions
Black olives for starry, Astrid eyes
Could that really be her?
(Silver sedan exits from parking lot)
The number eighty-seven
Somewhere on its license plate

A leviathan thirty yards offshore
Two young men
One with broad hips standing
Me in wetsuit and weight belt
Crawling south
I don't surf
Fiddler crabs from heaven

"Let her in"
By a grandfather clock
Next to French doors
In front of a painting
Handed over by a surgeon's family

When someone or something calls you a terrorist
You take pause
"Don't you have any empathy?"
The brand of which was offered me
Probably
Came too late
The damage done…
Harm…
I can't explain…
But I bet you can
And would like to someday

"I'm a big fan; release it all"
I'd taken the cure and just gotten through

Ninety days and a fireworks display with climax
On Surfside Beach
A vision of your happy pappy
Suffering his own smile
You can imagine how I felt

No … you can't imagine
'Cause things would be different

Sad news
I guess it's your turn to cry awhile
The rhythm you said you weren't feeling
Face down
Dust talk in your room after the war
"Is anybody home?"
I guess it's *my* turn to cry a while…
Again
Throwing jelly beans into the air
At the open mic on Oak Street
She turned slowly
Made of white cloud
Will I ever see her this way again?

"Hi…"
At Jimmy's Diner
Where we first met thirty-one years ago
By the back counter
Your legs crossed
One ankle wrapped around the other

A vision of the cupping and flick of a wrist
At the foot of my bed

You knew what you were doing, woman
It led to my last vow

At Manolo's
With one of your grown children
You in pink dress and fingerprints
Doing the "Itsy Bitsy Spider"

In the Navarre supermarket
Rust orange-lit chrome-copper eyes
Head rolling back
My approach
Plastic packaging
Choices

Fooling around on the sidewalk
On the way to work
Braid thick, tight, and high

Standing by the paperbacks
In a French Quarter pharmacy

Henry in blue convertible
Henry with blowtorch years before
Henry on sidewalk
Me on bike

Henry in the Grove wearing fuchsia scarf
Henry landscaping on San Pablo
Henry in purple Mustang
Henry going down on you
Henry on Atlantic Boulevard
At the top of the state of Florida

Someone left a Mohammed Ali / Sonny Liston
  t-shirt
A tall raspberry Arizona Iced Tea can
And broken glass
At the pool
A crystal halo
Really?
Yes, really

In the back of a Walgreen's
The dance continues
EST drivel
"One-step"
In front of the liquor store
You in black and gray
I heard you cry that night

Touching your toe in the apartment
You jumped
From snoring lightly

Keebler's cookies
French doors
New Year's Eve confession
I can't remember that Japanese dude's name
But I remember the silly song he sang

What you talkin' 'bout?
You don't like reggae music!
What you talkin' 'bout?
You don't like reggae music!

Every time something the least bit negative happened
He would say "Natty dread strikes again"
And he'd walk around town
Strummin' his guitar
Meh-meh…
We sat at a table
You wore a mauve linen shirt
I said I liked the fabric
He said, "I think it's sexy"

You laughed when the oil and vinegar spilled out on
    my plate

"What's taking so long?"
From a Jacksonville bathtub
The sign in front of your family's house

Yellow letters
White sign
Classic Citröen in the garage

On the bus with telephone and diamond studs
What's your name?
Ravi

Two zombies on the sidewalk
On Crespi Drive

Don't worry
Don't get upset
On a Biscayne Point walkway
Waiting limousine full of swap-shop garbage

Self-respect
Okay, Josephine

"Pathetic"
A recent message I haven't anchored into yet
A little lady in a tan Bentley on Brickell Avenue
License plate—SHVA PCE
Vered plays piano on 9th in Bavli

That girl with missing teeth
And cardboard smile
By a tree in Tel Aviv

The strange woman chasing pigeons
On a rooftop at dawn in Turin
Or was it Milan?

Wonder-dog in black slit sweatpants
On Alton Road

"It's embarrassing…
Which party if not all?"

On National Public Radio
"Hi, I'm Smadar…
Go play"
The textures and sounds of an oversexed voice

Doorway across the hall
Parting glances
Our usual…

Leaning against the wall on Royal
In the aftershock

Lemons

Razors

Wha…?

Sports Illustrated Swimsuit Edition in gauze

Oh yeah…

At Penn station

Arriving in New York after twenty-five years of
absence

Again

Costume shades

She turned around and ran to Dunkin' Donuts

A stolen kiss from Slim Henry in Central Park

The twang of a sword

Vibrating in the air

Thoughts of what intelligent agency females go
through…

Buttoning up your fatigues in a bedroom

Adjusting yourself on a motorcycle seat

An infant in the bedroom

Crawling around haphazardly

Detective Heart

Is that you?

Seen it on Fuller Street and St. Charles
Walking back to the boarding house
On a Sunday afternoon
Something called my name
A wavering Andromeda

The little girl in Baka
Turning and running on gravel
Scared
Entering a duplex through the screen door

I sat and watched as much of the movie *White Sands*
   as I could bear
A child who could have been your sister
What's he doing?
Where's he going?

Whatever citronella jaundice is
You caught it somewhere in the northeast
"Why don't you stay over?"

At an intersection in Jensen Beach, Florida
With reflectors on your eyes
You wore blue leggings
I complimented you on your strange bicycle
It may have been in Stuart County … I'm not sure

Woman, I don't recognize you, mostly
But I knew it was you by your hairline
Under the white sun
In that dirty, dusty Louisiana town
I was fading off to sleep
When a voice said, "I can't go on…
Go to the market"
But it ain't anybody's business
None of this is, come to think of it

And the other night
Jet-ski
Rickenbacker Causeway
There are a thousand ways to say, "I'm sorry"

Shiny Pantene hair
Stepping back with PJ from the couch
Was it something I said?

The government over there
Labeled your first husband a 'drug addict'
He's gutsy on crutches
Got to give him that much
He'll take it anyhow
Thank God a man is falling through a trap door

Your aquamarine Danskins
Showed a foot big enough to step on me

The girl in the shawl
Handing out sesame candies to children
In a faraway place

The same year
Returning to New Orleans
The bus driver knew
That I'd ejaculated over a dream
With the underage porn star, Tracy Lourdes, in it
What a mess!
I was nineteen once
Grayhound bus drivers have seen it all

Last night
The common white two-door
Driven by a woman
Who stopped and turned her head to me
Sitting under the MetroRail
In the well-lit walkway
"I never knew how much you wanted to be a widower"
Spoke she in the sun with brown socks to her knees
    and shorts on

The lookalike in the laundromat
The news reported someone dancing on the roof of
   the embassy
An adult in a petting zoo cage
With her head held back
Leif Ericson outside a strange mound of soil
I thought of northeastern Australia

I never walked away proud
I never walked away pleased
I never dumped anyone to bring hurt
I never dumped anyone … period

I've been called a coward and a bastard
And other names so simple
I could open a hardware store
My failure so remunerated
I could work in the kitchen renovation department
The faux stainless is in
By the time the heralded simpletons
Figure out what "behavioral despair" means
Church bells will ring from Kansas City to
   Massachusetts
Effortlessly tolling somehow
Feels like laying hold of something big
The concentration of time within whispered vows

Being buried and dug up
Hatred…
The only thing that lasts, angel heart

The are spiders the size of parade floats
Stroking their featherlike cilia
Nothing like those fiddler crabs on a skewer
Elvis cassettes and coffins
One must live to fit in his old wetsuit
The sea is black
The rain is heavy
What of the Ural mountain range?
A pretty people would be born
For those spreading out
South of Ethiopia

I know someone who's turned father against son
Son against father
Over and over again
For the sake of symmetry
Not in the name of love
Emmys and Oscars in the corners on the floor
Unhinged half-collapsed doors
Broken windows
Stacked newspapers…

Where?

There…

In Kennedy Park

With your man at your side

You in Izod

Blue and white-striped

With a strange, barbed washer

Loosely falling in the shirt's print

A surfboard-sized grunion-amoeba wallowing
   there on the Vita-course

Three of us walked south

You stopped and turned into me

Someone screamed…

Or yelled…

Or both

I woke up

There's a shortish woman

Who, at lunch hour

Tucks her hair back

And straps on rollerblades

And takes Deco Drive by storm

Boot over boot

She leans into it like she means it

Speedskater form

Maybe you've seen her

Amongst the architecture

Roller girl

Let's a taxi graze her hip

Toro toro, taxi

See you tomorrow, my son

She's got a seven-car garage

She hunts

She spies

Dudette major

Hep C

Sepsus

Tetanus

Put your hand on my head, baby

Do I have a temperature?

Elusive partner

The arrow's tip

The arrow's feather

Fourteen parishes

Maple leaves

Its like rain on your wedding day

Don't know what "all right" even means

If the Bible is right, the avocado is a blunder

Back in the war

Jackie Frasier

Through all of this

I haven't used the word "nemesis"

I lit a candle

There was a presence when I began to read the
man's lyrics

Just twenty miles out of Los Angeles

Someone said, "Beyond the first few miles

You're usually just a pain in the ass"

Aquarius

Sagittarius

Cancer

Pisces

Virgo

Leo

Libra

Aries

Taurus

Gemini

I hear the rising ends

Up there in the first depths of the sky

The experience of death is the same

But not the same for everyone

The timeless explosion of fantasy's dream
Marriage is the greater blessing
Don't let your baby down

Woe is me…
But woe is home to me
I can't say it's a pleasure to write all of this
What's that?
It's poetry
Who's that?
That's me
Somebody turned a framed picture
Face-down on their bedstand
Somebody is hot-headed and throws things
I'm sure he's a wild man

What is faith to the faithless?
Faith to the faithless is a papyrus plant
After spring showers
It'll be dark and cold before it dries
Retentive is blood's quality
A world tour's revenue

Where I'll find comfort
God knows

If you ever want to reach me
You'll know where to look

July 3, 2017
For sexual misconduct
A high-level priest in Australia
Is brought before a panel that includes the Pope,
   himself
Another nightclub has been shot up
This time, in Little Rock, Arkansas
Loggerhead turtles with gross facial tumors
Are cared for in a Miami marine hospital
Wildfires rage in the west
Last week, two children drowned
In ungated swimming pools
An eight-foot cobra was hiding under a bed
A world away…
Jakarta or somewhere
What's Tom Cruise's ex-wife doing these days?

In gold
She held and used an orthopedic walking cane on
   the boulevard
A red convertible Corvette with a black top roared by
I passed her on my bicycle

Her lower lip luscious and kissable

Someone said, "I'm sorry I've messed everything up"

Someone in there lives on poetry

Someone whispered, "I like you"

I folded on the matt in my living room

Saying, "Please … *please…*"

A woman holding off an elderly gentlemen in

a garage

She

Laughing

Them

Shuffling their steps

I heard Woodrow Wilson's guns

I heard them in the harbor[12]

Isla Papel, Papel Isla

The islands house people
Who can't eat the fish no more
The islands unload chemical waste
For $2.40 an hour

You might think that the islands are filled
With people of wholesome thought and gentle speech
And they are…
The islands are filled with people of wholesome
   thought and gentle speech
But black-on-black crime you'll surely find there
The same proving grounds
Piss in the streets

The islands…
One love
One heart
Let's get together and feel all right
Bermuda
Bahamas
You need *serious* security
Way up in the Virgin Island heights

"Sir Lithgow, sir
  The islands are so very pleasant this time of year
  The cool breezes might help you to relax again"

"Oh yes, Bagley
  Wouldn't that be something splendid?
  To relax again?"

"Sir, should I call the Ocean Club
  And make a reservation?"

To fly in on a jet plane
Siesta
Cabana
All those fresh white towels
Steel drums
White rum
Cranberry and vodka

One time, I asked my friend, Rasta Rick…
I asked him, "Ricky…
What would it be like to walk around the entire
  island of Jamaica?
Or Martinique?
Or Antigua?
Or Tobago?

What kind of challenge would it be?
What kind of people would I meet
If I ever did choose to wander
Cove to cove
Beach to beach?"

Rasta Rick replied
"Maiche, if ever you decide to do such a thing
Walk with nothing but the clothes on your back
And Maiche…
It's the third world out there
Dem say…
Trust no shadow after dark
You can step it out, Maiche
Step it out playin' on your harp"

And Rasta Rick continued
"The fruit in the grove
Don't pick it
That is somebody's rent
Nothing much is saved here, Maiche
And nothing much is earned
So nothing much is spent"

"Ricky, you mean to tell me that as I wander around
the island

People won't greet me with wreathes of flowers
And welcome me into their homes
Where the tables are filled with culinary delights
Spiced by the bird pepper tree?
And you mean their daughters so lovely and tall
They won't welcome me in with sugar cane
   and guava
To pass the hours?
I hear at dawn there's choral singing
And again when the sun goes down in the evening"

The youth…
The youth can be as vicious
As any knife-wielding, glue-sniffing lot anywhere
The shoeless and shirtless standing around
That yellow-eyed stare
The idea of a well-rounded diet hasn't happened
   everywhere
Many a dirty deed has gone down
Machete crazy
Runnin' though town

"Sir Lithgow and Mr. Bagley
  How nice it is to see you again
  And how lovely it is that you've chosen to stay
    with us once more

Hasn't it been a few years…?

Our island is certainly graced by your presence,
  gentlemen

And you know our resort welcomes you back with
  utmost sincerity

I'm sure you'll find the improvements we've made
  in our entertainment offerings…

Ahem, ahem…

  To be to your liking

  And holding great youthful appeal"

Ban De Soliel

San Tropez

Try the shrimp scampi

Sir, another cocktail?

The Cobb salad?

The acquired taste of quail

Warm sun

Cool breeze

Sandaled feet

Politics

Airstrips

Keep $300 in twenties

Scattered in different pockets

Three o'clock roadblock[13]
Cop
Always lookin' for "tips"

Rasta Rick said he lived on the Big Island in Hawaii
For six or seven years
Hawaii
Where the ground's made of flint
And the great bamboo grows high and thick
"Maiche, it's another breed of *everything* there
Baboons on the back roads
Wildcats
The centipedes can pierce your hide
Things happen quick!
Look here where I got bit"

Bananas got the tarantula
Sugar cane got the black king snake
Stir-fry the goat with a spoon, not a spatula
And coconut milk don't clot
Neither does the soy milk you've got
Just give it a shake

An island is a mountain surrounded by water
An island is a mountain surrounded by water
An island is a mountain surrounded by water

An island is a mountain surrounded by water
The islands house people
Who can't eat the fish no more
They unload chemical waste
For $2.40 an hour

You might think that the islands are filled
With people of wholesome thought and gentle speech
And they are…
The islands are filled with people of wholesome
    thought and gentle speech

And there's a choir at dawn and a choir at dusk
What a man can't do with a coconut husk
A boy in the market selling ripe tomatoes
What does the ghetto produce?
What kind of revolutionaries?
What kind of heroes?

  Come, Come
  Buy my tomatoes
  Come, Come

  Come, Come
  Buy my tomatoes
  Come, Come

Firearms and tourist barns and political upheaval
Airports and taxis and your luggage's retrieval

"Sir Lithgow, isn't it such a special, special thing
To be amongst the lovely people, living free?"

"Yes Bagley
Well spoken, man
And I think I'll have one more sherry
Before it's off to bed for me"

"Bottom's up, sir"

"Cheers"

"To the islands this time of year"

NEW YORK

I love New York

People stealing kisses on benches in the park

After a rainy night

All the trees are blackened, dark

I stood in line for coffee

With a dude in Coke bottle glasses

I'd say he read a lot

People in New York can be kind and smart

There had been an election

A loose parade

Poster boards

Bullhorns

It didn't feel like much of somethin' to be a part of

A dim afternoon in November

I love New York City

Washington Square

Battery Park

The lions in front of the library in there

The trees orange and yellow

A mild hallucination

I love New York in the early morning

When it's still

Quiet

Cold and clear

I chased the sun block-to-block

Hands in my pockets

Breath in the air

A mountain range in the center

I don't know how the streets run

I don't live there

Took the subway

Got on a bus

A dozen taxis

My new sneakers didn't fit

Now *there's* a New York crisis

Didn't eat any junk food

They've got it all there

Bra-less fourteen-year-old models stare

On sixty-foot screens canvasing Times Square

Popeye's fried chicken

The McRib is back!

Arby's lit up like no other Arby's anywhere

New York

An endless fair

Behind two inches of glass

Cartier?

Carty-*air*

Julliard School of Music
Kids with cello cases
Big as a Lazy Boy chair
Ground Zero is awesome for its girth
At night the water's like ghosts
Flowing back to earth
(respectfully)

In New York City
All the men are well dressed
All the girls are pretty
The cost in dollars
Of one single night in a midtown hotel:
Seven hundred and fifty
Hey, that's what it is at the heart of New York City
The Knicks at Madison Square Garden
Forest Hills for the US Open
The Yankees at Yankee stadium
Y' know the Dodgers were once from Brooklyn?

Outta nowhere one morning
I was walking
And I spied an old friend
"Hey gosh, its been so long…
How y' been?
You were so good…

Keep singin'"
It is rumored that there is a brick house
Where on a shelf, the Holy Grail lies
Beneath that bridge
I've seen both Olivia and Stabler
Goren and Eames
Even Rizzoli and Isles

It was about here that Charlie Brown's ropes
    cut loose
And he floated away
David Letterman's farewell fireworks display
Was right here on Broadway
I saw Danny Aiello on Madison and 26th
I thought he was dead!
Winona Ryder in her Pajamas, getting her paper
Shock of black hair
So unruly on her head

It's hard times in New York town
If you ain't got a few hundred grand to throw
    around
Hard times
The bicycle couriers are all published writers
The cab drivers were once doctors in
    Wherethefuckistan

Two jobs — He's always had two jobs
Two jobs makes ends meet
Keeps the roof on
Two jobs keeps his world spinnin' 'round

Thirty hours on a Greyhound
From Pensacola to here
Two hours by air
I'll need a Whole Foods Market
Soon as I get there
There's one on 56th and Columbus
My dehydrated peaches and pears

Mid-November
My favorite time of year
I'll make a return trip
Yeah
Stay over a week
That'd be hip
Astor Place for a clip
New York
New York
I'll write a poem one day...

THEY KEPT DRIVIN', TOM

They kept drivin', Tom

They kept drivin'

Must be the nature of the beast

'Cause they kept drivin'

Till the last cent was lost

Doin' it so mean

They kept on drivin'

Any day now I shall be released

They kept drivin', Tom

Turnin' the screw

Longtime comin'

Longtime gone

The definition of "chasm" is "A profound difference

    between people

Viewpoints

Feelings

Et cetera"

A chasm is…

They kept drivin', Tom

Up over the rail and into the river

The giver told the taker

That the taker was no giver

They sang "Danny Boy" at his funeral
She wore red to the service
Have I a thought that hasn't been repossessed?
It don't pay much
But there's a welcoming position
At the pharmacy on 76th

They kept drivin', Tom
Drivin'
Midnight at the oasis
Sometimes y' got t' let the pieces fall into
   their places
Sometimes y' got t' wait to see what
   happens next is
Sometimes y' got t' cut your losses
What can be done?
Closet cases

They kept drivin', Tom
Standin' him up
Knockin' him down
Standin' him up to knock 'im down again
Tom, they kept drivin'
Dear Prudence
Shine on you crazy diamond
He prayed to die on the day she'd die

Did sweet William for Barbara Allan

What was at length was a game with no rules

A game with no rules never ends

She impregnated herself in serial fashion

Paint dries

Blood thins

How to follow yourself out of difficult dreams

Cisterns and fountains and pools and springs

They kept drivin' him

Ridin' him

Duplicating and dividing him

Something here you find interesting?

I question myself on the refusal of blessing

That's not me…

But then again …

That *is* me

I *am* him

You took to corrections

You took to the reprobate

I was something convenient to meddle with

Let them eat pie

Let them eat cake

Sixteen years…

I spy your face

There lies the chasm
Sometimes you're better off not knowing how
    much you've been had
There was a line in a movie last night…
Something the founder of McDonald's said
About having to stand alongside certain people
When you'd rather be dead
I'll have to watch it again
The horror of this exclusion…
The atrophy
Falling at the feet of your enemy
Fighting revelation
They kept drivin'

Drivin'
Whatever politics you follow
You can follow too close
Am I the one who was so hard to get rid of?
Or am I the one who's always coming out of things
Smelling like a rose?
They kept drivin', Tom

ENDNOTES

1. Van Zant, Steve, "I've Been Waiting Such a Long Time"
2. Dylan, Bob, "Political World"
3. Dylan, Bob, "I and I"
4. Dylan, Bob, "The Disease of Conceit"
5. The Dixie Cups, "Iko Iko," 1964
6. Dylan, Bob, "Where Are You Tonight?"
7. Petty, Tom, "Let Me Up; I've Had Enough"
8. The Beatles, "Eleanor Rigby"
9. Hiatt, John, "Missing Pieces"
10. Dylan, Bob and Petty, Tom,"Band of the Hand"
11. Lightfoot, Gordon, "I've Got a Name"
12. Zevon, Warren, "Veracruz"
13. Marley, Robert, "Three O'clock Roadblock"

CPSIA information can be obtained
at www.ICGtesting.com
Printed in the USA
FSHW011234181020
74884FS

9 780997 575736